Late Medieval Irish Law Manuscripts:
A Reappraisal of Methodology and Context

ROWENA FINNANE

This study is aimed towards questioning the received view that the Irish law manuscripts produced in the secular law schools of the late medieval period are the work of antiquarians. It argues for an examination of the texts in their political, social and cultural contexts and particularly in relation to the Irish revival of the fourteenth century and onwards. In exploring the importance of interpretation in keeping an old text relevant in the present, the work examines the 'formalist' notion of legal interpretation, to which, it is argued, both the late medieval jurists and the scholars of the received view subscribed. An examination is provided of the way in which the glossing and commenting of the late medieval jurists may be seen as important in establishing the authority of the 'canonical' legal texts and in allowing for change: the way, in other words, the law manuscripts seek to resolve the tension between stasis and change.

The study also examines the importance of the manuscripts to legal education, and argues that this importance is another reason for questioning the assumed 'antiquarian' nature of the later jurists. It further argues that the manuscript activity of the jurists is inseparable from the connections between the jurists, their schools and the political élite of late medieval Ireland; and it examines the uses of the past in providing legitimacy and authority particularly in a legal context. The conclusion of this work is that there are sound reasons for believing that the manuscript activity of late medieval Irish jurists was not the antiquarian pursuit claimed by the received view, but was an activity very much centred in the present.

LATE MEDIEVAL IRISH LAW MANUSCRIPTS:
A REAPPRAISAL OF METHODOLOGY AND CONTEXT

ROWENA FINNANE

Sydney Series in Celtic Studies 13
The University of Sydney
2013

Published in Australia by
THE CELTIC STUDIES FOUNDATION
THE UNIVERSITY OF SYDNEY

in the
SYDNEY SERIES IN CELTIC STUDIES

ISBN: 978-1-74210-308-2

Cover illustration: Folio 21v of Royal Irish Academy MS 23 P 3 (now 1242), by permission of the Royal Irish Academy © RIA. The page shows text, gloss and commentary on the law tract *Ántéchtae* (viewable at www.isos.dias.ie and transcribed in *Corpus Iuris Hibernici* IV 1251.34–1254.15).

Foreword

The modern study of medieval Irish law has had an interesting history. In the eighteenth century, the motivations for collecting and publishing fragments of the legal materials were largely antiquarian, and the results highly speculative and of questionable value. In the nineteenth century, Ireland was caught up in a wider European nationalism which saw the publication of 'ancient laws' in many jurisdictions. The work of O'Curry and O'Donovan (on what became the *Ancient Laws of Ireland*) was thorough, and based on a knowledge of the language, albeit the study of Old Irish was in its infancy. However, O'Curry, in particular, tended to be overly credulous of the historical accuracy of myths about Ireland's glorious past in the manuscripts he translated. The ensuing period saw an interest in the laws that was motivated by pragmatic politics, and the push for Irish independence; a motivation that coloured even the work of that great scholar Eoin Mac Neill. For two generations in the twentieth century, the interest in the laws was largely philological; the study of Old Irish had been put on a scientific footing, and Thurneysen and Binchy mined the earliest layers of the laws. Their motivation was backward looking; their gaze was on the distant Indo-European past. Not surprisingly, this was a viewpoint that they projected onto their materials. Those studying the Old Irish laws for what they can reveal about the language and institutions of much older civilisations will not unnaturally tend to seek out and emphasise, perhaps over-emphasise, the archaic aspects of their material. For them, the linguistically more straightforward, and legally more elaborate, writings of the later middle ages will have little interest. Indeed, their lack of interest bordered on the contemptuous at times.

The 1980s saw the beginning of a re-examination of the early Irish laws of the seventh and eighth centuries. In particular, the view that they were peculiarly archaic, and based on an oral tradition preserved since before the coming of Christianity, has given way. It has been replaced by an appreciation that the early laws were the product of dynamic times, in which the Irish Church had the motivation and the resources to produce massive, de luxe collections of written laws that would buttress its legal interests. This growing realisation of the practical value, and contemporary nature, of the earliest written laws has only slowly begun to see a greater interest in the writings of later jurists, and a re-appraisal of their motivations and historical value. This has been a long time coming.

It is not surprising that the study of the later materials has been relatively neglected. Legal materials are often very complex, and rarely riveting to those whose focus is not legal. The Irish law tract *Bretha Étgid* contains a long commentary on injuries caused by accident and negligence in a blacksmith's forge. To those uninitiated in metalworking and law, it may appear to be a confusing welter of unreal facts and surreal legal distinctions. B. G. Scott, however, with his expert knowledge of medieval metalworking, found in it an astute guide to the dangers of medieval blacksmithing, written by someone remarkably well-versed in the realities and practicalities of that trade ('An early law tract on the blacksmith's forge', *Journal of Irish Archaeology* 1 (1983) 59-62). Jade Harman, with her thorough training in modern law, has more recently examined the commentary (in a work not yet published) and found it to be a faithful application of the medieval Irish law of causation and liability for harm.

Rowena Finnane's fine analysis of the nature, production and uses of the late medieval Irish legal manuscripts represents a similar act of illumination. It is no surprise that her analysis is likewise informed by a deep immersion in the nature, production and uses of the texts of modern law. To this she has added collaborative evidence garnered from a study of the treatment of late Roman and medieval English legal texts. Her book is a clear example of the importance of legal expertise in appreciating and interpreting legal material.

Finnane's account was completed as a Masters thesis in 1991. At the time, it was on the cutting-edge of the re-examination of late medieval Irish legal material. Very little of its bite has been dulled. Certainly, open contempt for the later legal writers is no longer fashionable, and they are starting to gain the respect that they deserve. But this will be a long process; the materials are complex and difficult. And nowhere else will you find as thorough an account of the legal value of the later medieval manuscripts as you will find in the present book. Finnane's account is informed by practical legal expertise, by a grasp of legal and literary theory, and by a clarity of thought and argumentation indicative of someone trained to present a case clearly, coherently and convincingly.

Neil McLeod
17 May 2013

Editor's note

This book was originally a Master's Thesis submitted in the Faculty of Arts at the University of Sydney in 1991. It was to be published as Volume 3 in the Sydney Series in Celtic Studies in 1992. Unfortunately, lack of funds prevented its publication at the time. The Celtic Studies Foundation is pleased to now have the funds available to publish this work. If others have shed light on this subject in the intervening years the author regrets the work does not show the benefit of it. She offers it now for any insight it may yet give to those present and future scholars and other persons interested in medieval Irish law and its transmission.

Contents

I. INTRODUCTION

Learn every old precedent here, though it be an old precedent it is not objectionable; it is on its premise you will best give judgment if you consider every aspect, I believe.

Advice given by Giolla na Naomh Mac Aodhagáin to the student of law, c. 1300 in Máirín Ní Dhonnchadha, 'An Address to a Student of Law', in O Corráin, Breatnach and McCone (eds.), *Sages, Saints and Storytellers: Celtic Studies in Honour of Professor James Carney,* An Sagart, Maynooth, 1989 p. 169.

In the field of late medieval Irish studies it is the received view that Irish legal manuscripts, produced in the secular law schools largely between the fourteenth and seventeenth centuries, were the work of antiquarians,[1] and as such had little relation to the legal realities of their day. It is a view that has been strongly argued by a small group of scholars throughout this century, and is one that has been accepted and perpetuated by many others. The aim of this study is to show that there are well-founded reasons for questioning this view. I will argue that there are grounds for a belief that the later medieval Irish jurists, far from being the purveyors of antiquarianism, were engaged in an activity very much centred in their present.

THE IMBALANCE IN THE WRITING ON THIS PERIOD

It is true that for post-Norman Ireland – Ireland say from 1170 to 1600 – we have a fair amount of good modern historical writing. If you examine it, however, you will find that about eighty per cent of it is based on Norman and English sources.[2]

This conclusion, arrived at several decades ago, is still fairly accurate. A considerable amount of the writing about late medieval Ireland focuses

---

[1] I base my use of the term 'antiquarian' on the sense of a concern with, or use of, the past for the past's sake; as an activity divorced from the present.

[2] John V. Kelleher, 'Early Irish History and Pseudo-History', *Studia Hibernica* 3, (1963) p. 116.

on Ireland in the context of its relationship with England, an approach which is valid to the extent that it deals with the unarguably important English presence in Ireland. However, the strong tendency toward perceiving late medieval Ireland as existing predominantly within this framework is unbalanced and misleading since this view reductively implies that all events and institutions in Ireland are the results of English acts and policies.[3] This view excludes a consideration both of native Irish society in terms of outside European influences, and also of the extent to which this Irish society was a continuation or revival of the complex political, legal and social systems that existed before the Anglo-Norman invasion.

A dramatic example of the scholarly acceptance of this perception is a comment by Curtis and McDowell in their introduction to *Irish Historical Documents 1172–1922.* They say that:

> [p]urely Gaelic sources, which reflect an archaic order of law, custom and institutions far removed from the normal medieval, and still more from modern, European civilisation, are a world to themselves and must be left to the experts in this rare field of learning.[4]

The 'Gaelic' element of late medieval Ireland is thus conveniently marginalised into a self-contained world existing both geographically and culturally on the periphery of Europe. It may accordingly be studied in isolation, with little regard to any interaction that this 'Gaelic' element might have had with other elements in later medieval Ireland. Being archaic, it is of little interest in comparison to the dynamic presence of the Anglo-Normans in Ireland. The danger of this imbalance, however, is that it can lead to the obscuring of native Irish society which, crucially, was dominant at certain times during this period. Much of the recent historical work on this period emphasises the complex relationships between the Irish and Anglo-Irish particularly after the fourteenth century. This work argues that the world of the native Irish was not a separate one: it cannot and should not be ignored. Nor, as I hope this study will show, was it necessarily a backward and archaic one.

---

[3] Katharine Simms, *From Kings to Warlords*, The Boydell Press, Suffolk, 1987 p. viii. In her preface she says that most textbooks on Medieval Ireland refer to the decline of the colony and the Gaelic resurgence, but concentrate on the political fortunes of the English Pale to the exclusion of the activities of the Irish chiefs and their newly acquired power.

[4] E. Curtis and R.B. Mc Dowell, *Irish Historical Documents, 1172-1922*, Methuen and Co. Ltd., London, 1943 p. 1.

My decision to study Irish law in the late medieval period is, then, partially a response to the perceived scarcity of material concerning native Irish society in the late medieval period as compared with the availability of material concerning the histories of the Anglo-Irish, Anglo-Norman, and English presences in Ireland during this time. But it is also a response to the scarcity of modern scholarly material available for the late medieval period in comparison with the material available on the institutions and culture of early medieval Ireland. According to J.A. Watt:

> ...the literature, laws, and institutions of early Irish society continue to attract attention, but their evolution in the later middle ages remains unstudied.[5]

This proposed neglect is particularly evident in the field of law. The study of native Irish law in the later medieval period has been, to a great degree, ignored. Mac Niocaill said over twenty years ago that 'Irish law in the later Middle Ages is almost completely unexplored'.[6] Apart from important scholarship carried out mainly by Mac Niocaill himself, Kenneth Nicholls, and more recently Katharine Simms and Nerys Patterson (and the treatment of the contact between Irish law and English common law by, for example, G.J. Hand), this statement remains true. I argue from the assumption that the history of the native Irish in later medieval Ireland, particularly within the context of law, is of interest and is worth studying.

THE IMBALANCE IN THE SOURCES

The imbalance in the attention to the history of the English and Anglo-Irish on the one hand, and the native Irish on the other, stems largely from a perception that the problems of the Irish sources are overwhelming. It is true that sources for English[7] rule in Ireland, from the Anglo-Normans to the Tudors, are more numerous, comprehensive, intelligible and accessible than those for the native Irish. Such English sources include judiciary rolls, state papers, administrative documents, statutes of the English and Irish

5 J.A. Watt, 'Approaches to the History of Fourteenth Century Ireland' in Cosgrove (ed.), A New History of Ireland II: Medieval Ireland, 1169-1534, Clarendon Press, Oxford, 1977 p. 306.

6 Gearóid Mac Niocaill, 'The contact of Irish and common law', N.I. Legal Quart., XXIII (1972) p. 16.

7 The use of this term is of course problematic. Different authors use the terms 'English', 'Anglo-Norman', 'Old English', 'Anglo-French' amongst others.

parliaments, literature and writings of Anglo-Irish and English people involved in some aspect of the colony/lordship, as well as some references in native Irish sources. The Irish sources are far more scant. The native Irish chiefs rarely kept administrative documents, and when they did they took little care with them.[8] Additionally, the Irish learned classes were not particularly attuned to the keeping of written records in the same manner as the English. The tradition of the literate élite was largely an oral one, and with little direct influence from Rome.[9] When the learned wrote, they wrote in Irish.

Nevertheless, while the Irish sources are fewer in number than the English, there remains a wealth of information still unexplored by modern historians. The main sources are the various Irish annals, Gaelic poetry (particularly bardic poetry, much of which has not even been edited), church documents, references in English documents (both statutes and other administrative sources), and references in the writings of Englishmen and others on the Irish, Irish history and travel. And there exist, of course, the complex and compelling Irish law manuscripts of principal interest to this study. It is undeniable that each of these sources has its drawbacks, if only because many of them are written in the Irish language.[10] Yet it would seem reasonable to suggest that any source of history is at best problematic in its ability to reveal the events of the past. In this work I will address some of the drawbacks said to make the Irish legal sources difficult to use in the study of the late Middle Ages.

THE LAW TEXTS

The law manuscripts are represented as being at least of dubious value, if not almost entirely useless as a source for the late medieval period of Irish history. Their chief utility it is commonly thought, lies in what they can reveal about early Irish society and, beyond this, pre-literate Celtic society. This is a view I find difficult to accept. It is indisputable that the manuscripts present more than a few difficulties, yet this should not be seen as a justification for simply dismissing them as historiographical sources for this period.

From the fourteenth to the sixteenth centuries, we have a large number of manuscripts containing legal material. In fact, except for a

---

8   Simms, *From Kings to Warlords*, p. 1.

9   *Ibid.*, p. 1.

10   See *Ibid.*, pp. 1-9 for a detailed description of the problems of these sources.

twelfth-century manuscript containing two law texts,[11] all the surviving legal writing for all periods of Irish history prior to the seventeenth century is found in manuscripts produced after the thirteenth century. As Binchy observes in his introduction to his *Corpus Iuris Hibernici* the earliest extant manuscript is a copy produced 400 years after the original was compiled and the majority of manuscripts are written 600–800 years after compilation. Thus as Binchy points out, the only information we have about early Irish law in the seventh and eighth centuries is that which has been 'preserved' for us by the later medieval jurists producing manuscripts after the thirteenth century. That information is also in a form arranged by the late medieval jurists.[12]

Except that the Irish manuscripts are written in the Irish language and script, in format they are similar to late medieval Canon law and Roman law manuscripts, in that the Irish manuscripts consist of three distinct sections of legal writing. The principal section is the 'text' or ancient canonical writing, written in large lettering.[13] This 'text' is thought to have been composed in the seventh and eighth centuries. The nature of this writing varies in both quantity and style: in places we have no more than a sentence, a rubric, a word or two. It is either in obscure verse or clearer prose (which, it is said, is generally obscure only when it has been copied faultily by a later scribe).[14]

The majority of the legal writing in the manuscripts, however, consists of gloss and commentary. The earliest glosses are said to have been written in the eighth century,[15] many from the twelfth and the majority from after the fourteenth century. The glosses were written in a very small script, between the lines of the text and sometimes in the margins. They were added throughout the late medieval period. Glosses

---

11 Fergus Kelly, *A Guide to Early Irish Law*, Dublin Institute for Advanced Studies, Dublin, 1988 p. 249. This is in the manuscript Rawlinson B 502. Both texts are heavily glossed and one also has commentary.

12 D.A. Binchy, *Corpus Iuris Hibernici*, Vol. 1, Institúid Ard Léinn Bhaile Atha Cliath, 1978 p. vii.

13 See Francis John Byrne, 'Introduction', in Timothy O'Neill, *The Irish Hand*, The Dolmen Press, Dublin, 1984 for a description of handwriting and lettering: p. xv.

14 Mac Neill, 'Prolegomena to a study of the Ancient Laws of Ireland', *Irish Jurist*, 2 (1967) pp. 111-112.

15 Kelly, *A Guide to Early Irish Law*, p. 249. The manuscript H 3.18 contains glosses on the Senchas Már which can be dated to the ninth century. [See now Liam Breatnach, *A Companion to the Corpus Iuris Hibernici*, Dublin Institute for Advanced Studies, Dublin, 2005, p. 344.]

either give etymological explanations of the ancient text, taken word by word, phrase by phrase (a 'translation' of old text into more modern language); or offer a more lengthy 'explanation' of the text and its terms. Where they offer this 'explanation', glosses are somewhat like the commentaries, only shorter.[16]

The commentaries on the texts were added by many different scribes over a period of several hundred years. They derive mainly from manuscripts produced in the fourteenth to sixteenth centuries and are more lengthy dissertations appended by way of similar subject matter to the canonical writing. They are written in a medium sized text. The earliest is dated probably to the tenth century, although they include many quotations from a much earlier period – quotations as old even as the ancient texts.[17]

Thus what we have is an enormous amount of legal writing, most of it being studied and copied in the fourteenth to sixteenth centuries, but which has been regarded almost exclusively in terms of the earlier period. The glosses and commentaries are consulted for any information they contain concerning the earlier period, or assistance they might give to understanding that period. Any relevance to their own period remains critically unexamined. As a source for late medieval Ireland, the law texts are certainly problematic – often because of the difficulties of dating. There is no time scale for the glosses and commentaries as an aid to evidence of change: there are few linguistic clues by which to date them, and there is little evidence as to individual authors.[18] Nevertheless, part of the problem is that detailed study for this purpose has simply not been pursued – despite the obvious need for such investigation. Additional information, for instance, is readily available from the marginal comments made by scribes on the manuscripts they were transcribing. Unfortunately no extensive study of these has yet been published.[19]

---

[16] Simms, *From Kings to Warlords*, p. 1.

[17] Mac Neill, 'Prolegomena', p. 112.

[18] Gearóid Mac Niocaill, 'Aspects of Irish Law in the Late Thirteenth Century', *Historical Studies* X (1976) p. 29.

[19] For descriptions of marginalia see Standish Hayes O'Grady, *Catalogue of Irish Manuscripts in the British Museum*, Vol. 1, London 1926 and T. K. Abbott and E. J. Gwynn, Catalogue of Manuscripts, Library of Trinity College, Dublin, Dublin, 1921.

THE TREATMENT OF THE QUESTION

The treatment of Irish law in late medieval Ireland must initially be seen in the context of attitudes towards Irish society in this period. The commonly held view in our century is that Irish society in the late medieval period is of little interest. However, to begin a study of the treatment of Irish law in late medieval Ireland, particularly of the fourteenth to sixteenth centuries, by an exclusive examination of twentieth-century interpretations would be to ignore the origins of many assumptions contained in these interpretations, assumptions which often come from the late medieval era itself. Particularly from Tudor times onwards, when writing about Irish society in the English language markedly increased, much was written to suggest that Irish law was decayed and backward-looking, unchanged for hundreds of years and thus out of date and irrelevant. Tudor bias, propaganda and misapprehension of Irish law (and indeed of the Irish learned classes and Irish society generally) have continued to the present day, if in a somewhat changed form. The Irish lawyers are characterised as conservative, their scribal activity an antiquarian pursuit which did not allow the written law to change in sympathy with social and cultural change. They apparently did not understand the ancient texts but used them as part of the social and political pretensions of their profession.

In the twentieth century, attitudes towards pre-Norman Irish society establish the tone for the historical treatment of the whole Irish medieval period. Crucial to this treatment was the contribution of G.H. Orpen. Debate over the state of Irish society prior to the coming of the Normans was sparked by Orpen's 1920 series *Ireland Under the Normans*.[20] In an attempt to justify the Anglo-Norman invasion, Orpen described pre-Norman Ireland as divided into 185 tribes, all operating in a largely autonomous way in a land of intertribal fighting, outside the mainstream of European events.[21]

Orpen conceived of Irish law as archaic, having no regular machinery for legislating or for judicially enforcing customs normally observed in society.[22] The lack of Roman domination was, he said, the reason why the

---

[20] G.H. Orpen, *Ireland Under the Normans*, Clarendon Press, Oxford, 1920. (Reprinted 1968).

[21] *Ibid.*, p. 25-26. This claim has been challenged, and in many important respects has been disproven. See especially Donnchadh O'Corráin, 'Nationality and Kingship in pre-Norman Ireland', in *Nationality and the Pursuit of National Independence*, The Apple Tree Press, Belfast. 1978. pp. 1-35.

[22] Orpen, *Ireland Under the Normans*, p. 104.

Irish had failed to acquire the idea that the essential condition of a progressive society is a strong centrally organised state.[23] And as such, twelfth-century Ireland lagged far behind the progressive nations of Europe.[24] In nature it was essentially a static society whose institutions and laws had changed little from the classical period when the laws were first recorded in the seventh and eighth centuries, to the latest period of legal writing in the seventeenth century. He viewed the Irish legal system as an effective block on progress in a society characterised by anarchy. In accordance with this belief Orpen saw the material in the law manuscripts as descriptive of an unchanged society. He saw it as unlikely that 'elaborate dissertations on obsolete customs' would be copied into textbooks in the fourteenth century, and that purely antiquarian matter could be distinguished from matter of greater applicability; so that it can be assumed, Orpen argued, that the customs described in the commentaries were in full force in the twelfth century and indeed probably later.[25]

Orpen's position was attacked by Eoin Mac Neill. He sought to show that the Irish did indeed have a strong national government, with a complementary strong role for the king as legislator and as judicial enforcer of the law. However Binchy, for long the pre-eminent scholar in the field of early Irish law, says Orpen and Mac Neill 'started from precisely the same suppressed premise, that law and order were impossible in any society where the state had not substantially the same functions as the late Victorian era in which they both grew up'.[26] Binchy has shown, for example, that Mac Neill's claims about the High King of Tara have 'no more basis in law than in fact'.[27]

O'Corráin, in replying to the debate between Orpen and Mac Neill, shows that Ireland prior to the invasion was steadily moving towards national unity as the king gradually obtained greater legislative and judicial powers although, he argues, by the twelfth century these powers were not nearly as extensive as argued by Mac Neill.[28] The considerable political and social change of this period was generated not only by contact with the Vikings and Anglo-Normans across the sea, but from within Irish

---

23 *Ibid.*, pp. 105, 254.

24 *Ibid.*, p. 254.

25 *Ibid.*, p. 109

26 Quoted in O'Corráin, 'Nationality and Kingship ', p. 4.

27 *Ibid.*, p. 4.

28 *Ibid.*, passim.

society.[29] The hitherto fragmentary nature of Irish political organisation, which had largely been based on small localised power relationships, was shifting; distinct moves towards centralised political control became obvious. The units of political control became larger in scale as the number of rulers exercising ultimate political authority became smaller. By the tenth century there were no more than a dozen overkingships of any importance and there were significantly less by the twelfth.[30] According to O'Corráin, then, Irish society was in a state of flux; Orpen's 180 fragmented tribes have no basis in fact for this period. However, many of the assumptions underlying Orpen's work have been retained in a more refined way by later writers. The historical proposition of a decayed, backward looking legal system operating in an anarchic social environment, has seemingly prefaced most enquiries into the state of Irish law in pre-Norman and Anglo-Norman Ireland.

The broadest charge against the manuscript activity of the later Irish jurists, then, is that it is antiquarian in motivation; that it 'preserves' the texts of the past because of a mere love of the past. Binchy takes the view that Irish law in late medieval times, as revealed in the surviving law manuscripts, was largely an antiquarian study cut off from the great political and social changes taking place in late medieval Irish society. The laws as recorded after the introduction of Christianity received, according to Binchy, their final canonical form in the eighth century, from which date they were considered authoritative and immutable.[31] The lawyers were from that time 'prisoners of their own great past': a past described in the older law tracts showing, Binchy argues, a primitive, tribal society.[32] Binchy maintains that, in Ireland, the natural conservatism of the legal profession was taken to 'unheard of lengths'.[33] The task of the jurists was not to modernise the law in response to the political and social changes which had taken place in society of the day, but to learn by heart the ancient laws and to interpret them. This interpretation of the later medieval jurists was done through the glosses and commentaries and, in the opinion of Binchy, did not allow much scope for the reflection of social change.

---

[29]   Simms, *From Kings to Warlords*, p. 10.

[30]   O'Corráin, 'Nationality and Kingship', p. i1.

[31]   D.A. Binchy, 'Lawyers and Chroniclers', in Brian O'Cuív (ed.), *Seven Centuries of Irish Learning*, 1000-1700, Radio Eireann Thomas Davis Lectures, The Stationery Office, 1961 p. 59.

[32]   *Ibid.*

[33]   *Ibid.*, p. 60.

One of the results of this antiquarian activity, the received view argues, was that later jurists were unable to understand the language and institutions contained in the canonical tracts. Mac Neill argues that owing to the lapse in time between the first recordings of Irish law and the latest commentaries, there is a failure by the commentators to understand the older language in which the text is written, and a lack of familiarity with the ancient practices and institutions. This, Mac Neill asserts, suggests these practices and institutions had by then become obsolete.[34] Binchy proposes that the glosses are often the work of a later jurist trying to mask his ignorance of the archaic language of the older text with wild etymological guesses.[35] The commentaries, Binchy alleges, are 'an even greater disappointment'. Because, theoretically, the law could not change, the commentator could not even consider bringing the text up to date, much less criticising it: all he could do was interpret by explaining it in modern language, covering over with elaborate paragraphs his inability to understand an archaic sentence. The result, concludes Binchy, is that we can gain no understanding from these later jurists of how the law was operating in the later Middle Ages.

The other problem which Binchy alleges the jurists created for themselves stemmed from the fact that various law tracts originated in different schools and in different areas, and contained contradictory law on certain points. This led to 'flights of fancy' as much time was spent in a pointless attempt at reconciling them. The later Irish jurists continued to propagate the fiction that law was in perfect unity and that every rule was consistent with every other rule: when faced with differences between the older and newer sections of the tracts they would try to explain these away in their commentaries.[36]

But perhaps one of the strongest attacks on the commentaries in particular is that they are excessively casuistic; that they are quibbling and over-elaborate in their approach to legal problems. The prevailing casuistry is said to show that commentary was, once again, divorced from the legal practice and the society of the day. Binchy considers that Mac Neill was right to ignore the glosses and the 'fantastic interpretations' offered by the commentators.[37] He says that:

---

[34]   Mac Neill, 'Prolegomena', p. 113-114.

[35]   Binchy, 'Lawyers and Chroniclers', p. 61.

[36]   Binchy, 'Ancient Irish Law', p. 89.

[37]   D.A. Binchy, 'Irish History and Irish Law: II', *Studia Hibernica*, 16 (1976), p. 32.

...they weave a crazy pattern of rabbinical distinctions, schematic constructions, academic casuistry and arithmetical calculations, none of which has any value for the student of Irish legal history.[38]

This conclusion is supported by Thurneysen who claims that the work of the commentators produced:

an amalgam in which contact with the world of fact is abandoned in favour of elaborate calculations, minute casuistry, and strange constructions which often lead to quite impossible results and can never have had any significance for the practical administration of the law...the dreams of bookworms and pedlars of antiquarianism.[39]

Many of the received view argue that although the lawyers did not understand their texts, they used them as a source of prestige. Binchy asserts that in:

...medieval Ireland the lawyers owed much of their prestige to the fact that they were the custodians of ancient and arcane wisdom, and they naturally made great play with their archaic texts, being well aware that the layman would never guess how limited was their knowledge of these texts.[40]

Binchy says that the manuscript activity of the jurists was kept separate from the day-to-day business of the law.[41] Gearóid Mac Niocaill in a discussion of litigation in late Irish law, also takes up the issue of the law manuscripts as being part of the pretensions of the late medieval lawyers. He argues that the canonical texts were cited in litigation (and thus were involved in the practice of the law) but that as the jurists did not understand these texts, the citations bore little relation to the case to be decided, being of more utility in establishing the erudition of the lawyers.[42] David Dumville also emphasises that the later medieval jurists made use of canonical texts they did not understand as part of the trappings of the legal profession. He arrives at this conclusion in trying to explain the apparent discontinuity between the writing of the law texts on the one hand, and the glossing and commentary on the other. The discontinuity, Dumville says, is evidenced by the change in legal style. Dumville suggests that in the chaos following the aftermath of the Norse

[38] Quoted from his Rhys Lecture in *Ibid.*, p. 33 .
[39] Quoted in *Ibid.*, p. 32.
[40] Binchy, 'Lawyers and Chroniclers', p. 64.
[41] *Ibid.*
[42] Mac Niocaill, 'Notes on Litigation in Late Irish Law', pp. 299-307.

invasions, a whole generation of legal scholars and students was lost – possibly to the slave markets of Europe. The ancient texts then fell into the hands of antiquarians who valued them and wished to preserve them for the 'past' they contained but who failed to understand them. The law texts became not part of the method of the Irish legal profession, as a whole, but merely part of the pretensions of an élite within the legal profession, while everyday legal practice proceeded unaffected.[43] It should perhaps be pointed out that Dumville's distinctive approach assumes that the Norse invasions were more widespread than is usually accepted, and it also very easily equates a change in legal style with legal discontinuity of a radical kind.

It is critical, however, that many of the scholars cited above do on occasions allow that the later legal writing is not entirely antiquarian or casuistic. Mac Neill concludes that, owing to the conservatism of the Irish jurists and the veneration with which the ancient texts were treated, the inclusion of conflicting material shows weighty social pressure owing to the change in social usage.[44] Binchy modifies his views, and in his later writing concedes that some changes in society and structures are revealed in the works of the later jurists.[45] In his introduction to *Corpus Iuris Hibernici,* Binchy says that if the fictions of uniformity and immutability are ignored we can sometimes detect changes in rules and institutions.[46] Mac Niocaill allows that at least the commentaries had some connection with the case at hand when he shows that material from the law manuscripts, both ancient text and more modern commentary, were cited in litigation.[47]

But despite these partial concessions and qualifications, the received view on the state of Irish law, and more particularly legal writing in this period, is that it was an antiquarian pursuit. That is, legal writing was archaic, of little relevance to the society in which it existed, intensely conservative, almost entirely incapable of admitting change, serving only as part of the pageantry of the legal profession.

---

[43] David Dumville, 'Language, Literature and Law in Medieval Ireland: Some Questions of Transmission' *Cambridge Medieval Celtic Studies,* 9 (Summer 1985) pp. 97-98.

[44] Mac Neill, 'Prolegomena', p. 113.

[45] D.A.Binchy, 'Irish Law Tracts Re-edited: I. Coibnes Uisci Tharidne', *Eriu,* (1955) XVII, p. 52.

[46] Binchy, *Corpus Iuris Hibernici,* p. viii.

[47] Mac Niocaill, 'Notes on Litigation in Late Irish Law ', pp. 304-305.

A CHALLENGE TO THE RECEIVED VIEW: NERYS PATTERSON

In an article appearing in *Cambridge Medieval Celtic Studies,* Nerys
Patterson questions the 'received view that the function of late legal
writing was confined to legitimising the legal profession, and was devoid
of substantive meaning or instrumental value'.[48] It will perhaps be useful
to look at her analysis in detail as a preliminary to this study, which in
some ways adopts a similar approach.

Nerys Patterson addresses two questions. The first is the issue of the
validity of the assumption that Brehon Law was not applied in the later
medieval period. Patterson accepts Binchy's argument that none of the
surviving examples of Brehon judgments shows evidence of the use of
Brehon law. However she argues that the surviving examples are all
judgments involving the interests of the Old English nobility, and a few
Irish lords, in land. It is, she says, a limited area of law and not indicative
of the continuation of Irish law in other areas of social regulation. For
instance she refers to the thirteenth century document of Giolla na Naomh
Mac Aodhagáin which Mac Niocaill has described as 'close to the realities
of the thirteenth century' and also as a systematisation of rules with 'roots
in classical Irish learning'.[49] The development of a marcher law as
described by Mac Niocaill is, she argues, evidence of the vitality of the
Irish legal profession. This profession sought not the abandonment, but
rather the modification of legal rules in a society where Gaelic institutions
remained the de facto principles of social organisation until the final
military defeat in the seventeenth century.[50]

She further argues that the assumptions about late Irish law stem from
a lack of documentary evidence owing to a policy of convenient
destruction and neglect of manuscripts, and from the largely oral nature of
much of the Brehon legal proceedings.[51] Patterson says that lack of
evidence is used to prove the non-existence of something; that the received
view asserts that if you can not see it then it is not there. She is of the
opinion that the validity of this argument depends on there being reason to

---

[48] Nerys Patterson, 'Brehon Law in Late Medieval Ireland: "Antiquarian and
Obsolete" or "Traditional and Functional"?' *Cambridge Medieval Celtic Studies,*
17 (Summer 1989), p. 45.

[49] *Ibid.,* p. 46.

[50] *Ibid.,* p. 46.

[51] *Ibid.,* p. 48.

believe that positive evidence should exist – and she has shown that this is not so.[52]

The second question Patterson addresses is whether the assumptions derived from an examination of the legal style of the law tracts are valid. She challenges the accepted notion that the ancient law texts were once a coherent logical structure that has fallen into decay.[53] This, she says, has been accepted by historians as they attempt to explain the decay of institutions and production of law texts following the coming of the Vikings to Ireland. However she emphasises that it is a change in legal literary style that is at issue, not whether legal composition continued.[54] She rebuts, with examples, the conception that, in comparison with the glosses and commentaries, the early texts are clearer and more realistic. This, she claims, shows that the realism of the earliest tracts has been exaggerated in the same way that the fantastic nature of the later writing has been.[55] She proffers the alternative view that the changes in style adopted by the jurists in the manuscripts allow for greater flexibility in the interpretation of the written rules than would a developed body of systematised written law.[56] Nevertheless she insists that she is not saying that the later scribes fully understood the early tracts, but simply that the evidence presented does not prove the extent of their comprehension. She thus holds that there is reason to assume that they did understand much of the early texts, and continued to manipulate these for their own purposes.[57]

Patterson analyses the four major objections given as evidence for the archaism, irrelevance and antiquarianism of the later legal writing: that rules are open-ended; there is ambiguity in the legal writing; that the writing is schematic; and the use of etymologies. The situation in the manuscripts where two seemingly contradictory rules are cited as a solution to a legal problem, she says, is argued by the received view as an

---

52   *Ibid.*, pp. 47-48; See also R.R. Davies, 'The Administration of Law in Medieval Wales: The Role of the Ynad Cwmwd (Judex Patrie)', in T.M. Charles Edwards, Morfydd E. Owen and D.B. Walters (eds.), *Lawyers and Laymen*, University of Wales Press, Cardiff, 1986 p. 258. In Wales, as in Ireland, there is a lack of contemporary source documents from which to discover the operation of native law. And it is not only that they did not survive, but also that one would not expect them to have ever been written.

53   Patterson, 'Brehon Law in Late Medieval Ireland', p. 49.

54   *Ibid.*, p. 49.

55   *Ibid.*, p. 49.

56   *Ibid.*, p. 51.

57   *Ibid.*, p. 52.

example of the open-endedness of rules, and as a negative attribute of a legal system. Patterson replies to this by suggesting that this benefitted the jurist as he was not tied down to any precise definitions. He was consequently able to give a decision based on his own expertise as one versed in the law, with the greater freedom to give a decision which accorded with his sense of justice. Thus a jurist might combine a knowledge of contemporary community mores as well as the oral and written legal tradition.[58]

The ambiguity in the meaning of many of the texts is likewise condemned by the subscribers to the received view. Against this Patterson argues that indeterminacy was legally productive within a tradition that required open-endedness in its norm statements; indeterminacy leaves a tradition more open to changes in interpretation or details. In this open-endedness she says the Irish legal system is not inherently different from modern systems – Patterson cites Max Gluckman, the legal anthropologist, who points out that the leading western jurists say that even the most explicitly systematised law rests upon semantic uncertainties.[59]

In her reply to the charges of excessive schematism in the later legal writing, which is deemed a sign of declining standards, Patterson points out that schematism has been shown to be present in the oldest tracts, which are considered more realistic, and thus is not merely a feature of later legal writing. She further argues that schematism was a method prevalent in medieval law teaching. The practice of setting forth many examples through which a general principle may be deduced was as important a methodological approach in the formation of jural norms in English legal teaching in the period as in Irish. In fact she details many common elements in the two systems of the period, so that in the fifteenth century Irish lawyers were able to operate in both jurisdictions.[60]

The etymologising employed by the jurists, particularly in the glosses, has been considered decadent, illustrating the pedantry and incomprehension of the later jurists. While Patterson concedes that it is difficult to differentiate between the glossator's misunderstanding of a word and a decision to give an altered meaning to a word, she does argue that the copiousness with which etymology is practised in the texts is consistent with medieval scholarly ideals. These etymologies did not

---

[58] *Ibid.*, pp. 52-53.
[59] *Ibid.*, pp. 54-55.
[60] *Ibid.*, pp. 55-57.

necessarily have a role in legal argument, but were important in the transmission of legal ideas.[61]

Patterson offers three further ideas to support her argument. Firstly, that the meaning of the law texts was able to be influenced by jurists in relation to the way in which they selected and arranged pieces from various sources giving them control over the written as well as the oral interpretation of the texts.[62] Secondly, that the features that are argued as being evidence for the decay of legal writing in this time have largely been seen through an Anglocentric frame of reference which was first begun in the sixteenth century in an attempt to denigrate the law of the native Irish.[63] And finally, that lawyers held a prominent and respected position in society, and were often involved in major political events and thus were not cut off from the social realities of their society.[64]

Essentially, then, there have been three broad approaches to Irish law in the later Middle Ages. Orpen took the view, shared and elucidated by many after him, that the glosses and commentaries are largely explaining the older text. In stating that Irish society was static at least from the time of the Norse invasions, if not long before, he was able to say that the legal writing of the twelfth century and afterwards is a fair description of the customs and institutions of Irish society at the time. Binchy, Mac Neill, Thurneysen, Mac Niocaill and Dumville also take the view that the later legal writing is mainly only describing and explicating the older tracts. However, in seeing that Irish society had undergone great change throughout the period they thus conclude that this later legal writing can have no relevance to the later period because it does not clearly reflect changes in social reality. Patterson, in contrast to both of these approaches, argues that the later legal writing ostensibly deals with the older text, but that there is much in the way in which it does this to suggest this treatment of the older text also allows for change. Thus, in recognising that Irish society had changed in this time, she concludes that the law tracts may be of use, because they allow for social change to reflect itself within their discourse.

The received view firmly holds that the law manuscripts are antiquarian and reveal little of interest about the period – although most of the scholars who support this view do allow for at least a small amount of

---

61   *Ibid.*, pp. 58-59.
62   *Ibid.*, p. 59.
63   *Ibid.*, p. 60.
64   *Ibid.*, p. 61.

change in society to be revealed. This is, however, always directed towards discovering change in the substance of the law in a direct way. Nerys Patterson challenges the received view and says that we should assume that the law manuscripts allow for change and that the antiquarian element is the exception rather than the rule. The approach Patterson takes, and which I also take, is to look not at how the manuscripts show change in substance, but rather at how the method of the manuscripts allows for the law manuscripts to accommodate social and political change.

THE ISSUE OF 'TEXT'

Fundamentally this study is concerned with the issue of the text and how it is to be read. Eric Kline Silverman posits two opposed notions of 'text' which may be relevant here. One, an essentialistic view, argues that:

> ...a text has a real, true and objective existence. As an object, this text is constituted somewhat independently of its readers. It is created at a specific historical moment and continues to reference that moment as well as the author's intentions, regardless of the conditions surrounding its subsequent readings...[65]

The other argues that:

> ...a text exists only as a specific sociocultural creation, tied to events occurring at the time of reading. From this perspective, the text is constituted by both its authors and specific readers. It is therefore an individual-centred, subjective creation, not an objective external entity. The text is open ended yet historically framed, and its meaning is fashioned, as opposed to self-contained. [66]

The Irish jurists and those who argue the received view subscribe to the same essentialistic view of the text that the meaning of the text is self-contained. In the context of legal theory, this is a view which might be called, loosely, 'legal formalism'. The view assumes that governing any situation that may come before the law, there is a discoverable rule, objective and fixed in its legal meaning, so that it can be applied to the situation with certainty. Interpretation merely explicates and applies a fixed legal rule to a new fact situation. If interpretation is anything more, it

---

[65] Eric Kline Silverman, 'Clifford Geertz: Towards a More "Thick" Understanding', in Christopher Tilley (ed.), *Reading Material Culture: Structuralism, Hermeneutics and Post-Structuralism*, Basil Blackwell, Oxford, 1990 p. 152.

[66] *Ibid.*

opens the doors to subjectivity, which is seen as dangerous because social and political factors are allowed to become important. For the law to retain its authority it is necessary that the objectivity of the legal process be stressed; it must be seen to be removed from its social and political context. It is in this sense that the discourse of law fashions itself as an enclosed language system, the meanings of which are fixed without reference to the rest of society.

For the later medieval jurists the task was to maintain the existence of the text through the elaborate use of legal fictions and interpretative method, and through the argument that this use of legal fictions and method was in fact true to the original meaning of the text. The received view, although tacitly agreeing with the legal fictions, judges this task as a failure. The jurists did not maintain fidelity to the intentions of the legal authors, the glosses and commentaries are fancy and speculative, and so failed to recover the original and self-contained meaning of the texts. What remains for the modern scholar is, according to this formalist approach, the task of reconstructing as far as possible the 'original meaning' of the texts, either aided or unaided by the later jurists.

This study will take the alternative approach to the 'text' as defined by Silverman. In so doing it will suggest an alternative way in which the work of the late medieval jurists may be read. For if we see a more substantial role for interpretation, we may 'read' the mode of legal discourse manifest in the manuscripts not merely as antiquarianism, but as a present-centred activity inseparable from the society and political situation in which they were produced. It could thus be suggested that, for the world of the Irish jurists as much as for any other historical context, law is a '"register" of an actually existing language system'.[67] That, as language usage, it 'is a social practice and...its texts will bear the imprint of such practice or organisational background'.[68]

OVERVIEW OF THE ARGUMENT

In order to provide the historical frame for the further examination of our texts it will be useful to initially examine the manuscript tradition of the period together with a survey of the environs within which the law manuscripts were produced. My argument begins with an examination of

[67] Peter Goodrich, 'Law and Language: An Historical and Critical Introduction', *Journal of Law and Society*, Vol. 11, No. 2 (Summer 1984) p. 173.

[68] *Ibid.*, p. 174.

the relationship between the Irish revival of the fourteenth century onwards and the manuscript tradition. After a discussion of the tenth-, eleventh- and twelfth-century manuscript tradition, I examine the radically different environment in which the fourteenth-century tradition was being carried out, whilst in the same environment the fictions of a continuous and unchanging legal system were propagated.

It is said that the law manuscripts do not accommodate the social and political change which occurred in the years between the laws being written down and being glossed, commented on and recopied. That is, that they are preoccupied with the past, to the exclusion of the present. However, in my third chapter, I will be arguing that this view does not take full account of the scope for change through interpretation. This change allows for the continued life of the old text in the present. The glosses and commentaries were an interpretative technique, similar to those used in interpreting the Bible and later medieval Roman and Canon law. The technique is similar also to English common law, in that it rested on legal fictions which promoted the view that such interpretative activity was merely expounding the law, and certainly not changing it. Indeed, the authority for the changes wrought through interpretation relied upon adherence to these very fictions of unchanging meaning. This is one of the reasons I will be arguing that later medieval legal writing and arranging cannot be dismissed as the work of antiquarians; such a dismissal shows an excessive credulity for the fictions promoted by the very same texts which have been dismissed. Paradoxically, the received view which slights the jurists is itself largely determined by those jurists. If interpretative activity allows for change whilst maintaining the old text, it is an activity directed towards the present and the future.

Interpretation cannot occur without interpreters. And where such a major interpretative task is required to keep old law relevant in the present, there is a need for well trained interpreters. In the fourth chapter I examine in greater detail the nature of the legal education provided in the schools. One of the charges against the law texts, as we have seen, is that the texts are academic in their formulations, and casuistic. This, I believe, points to an important use for the law texts in late medieval Ireland: legal education. Because a well trained profession is essential to a workable legal system, this I would also argue makes the production of the law texts an activity centred in the present.

The glossing, commenting on, and copying of old texts, a group of activities all concerned with the past, is said to show the antiquarian tendencies of the later medieval Irish law schools. Contrary to this I would argue that this activity of the Irish jurists has deceived many of the received view. The methodology of the jurists themselves demands that we acknowledge the legal texts as the repositories of an immutable and continuous law, that we acknowledge the authority of the text, based as it is in the past. It is a legal methodology that directs our attention away from the later writing and toward the earlier authoritative text. Although the methodology of the texts requires that we regard them independently of their social and political context in late medieval Ireland, I believe they can, and should, be regarded within these contexts. This fixation with the past is very much based on present and future concerns; the law manuscripts use the past for the present. In the fifth chapter I will be arguing that the use of the past is significant in the claims it makes to legitimacy, and further that we cannot separate the production of law manuscripts and interpretative activity centred on the canonical texts on the one hand from the strong connections between the law schools and local ruling families on the other. I believe that there are valid reasons for questioning the assumption that the law texts are an antiquarian endeavour that exist only on an explicit level.

A NOTE ON THE USE OF TRANSLATIONS

A note must be made about the use of translations in this study. I am reliant upon the translations of others. An important drawback is that the fullest translation into English, *Ancient Laws of Ireland* (hereafter referred to as AL), was made last century when knowledge of Old Irish was limited. Thus there are many errors, particularly for the oldest sections. Mac Neill states that on almost every page there are inaccuracies and that the editors have failed to provide useful cross references and annotations.[69] Binchy says that what sometimes appears to be the ridiculous incomprehension of the later jurists often arises because in the official edition disagreement on a point of law by different glossators were printed as if they were by the same glossator.[70] However the translations of the Middle Irish and later Modern Irish sections, on which this study will be concentrating, are generally more accurate.[71]

---

69   Mac Neill, 'Prolegomena', p. 114.
70   Binchy, 'Irish Law Tracts Re-edited: I. Coibnes Uisci Thairidne', p. 54.
71   Binchy, 'Irish History and Irish Law: II', p. 14. See Mac Neill, 'Prolegomena', p. 114, Binchy, 'Irish Law Tracts Re-edited: I. Coibnes Uisci Thairidne', pp. 52-54 for more detailed discussion of the problems in translation of AL.

Where they exist I have used later, apparently more accurate translations. Of course translation in itself is problematic and will be discussed in a different context at a later point. Nevertheless the translations serve more to provide examples illustrating my main point. The study is directed toward an examination of the methodology of the law manuscripts and their social and political context and as such is not making a detailed analysis – in which situation translation would become more important than it is here.

II. LAW MANUSCRIPT PRODUCTION AND THE IRISH REVIVAL

This is the eve of Lady Day in Spring, and I grieve that from the Earl of Ormond's son Donogh O'Brien goes in danger of death. Also I am astonished that Carbry is courting counsel from Conor. The Park is my quarters. [Written by] Manus for Donall, who is himself travelling all over Ireland. A.D. 1567.

Marginal comment on an Ua Duibhdabhoireann manuscript. O'Grady, *Catalogue of Irish Manuscripts*, p.111.

If law is a 'register' of a particular language system the discourse of which, as language, will reveal the social and institutional background on which the law relies, it becomes crucial to examine the context in which this discourse took place. That is, before we take a closer look at the methodology in the legal discourse of the later medieval Irish jurists, it is important that we understand how the manuscripts related to the society in which they were produced. It is particularly significant, I will argue, that after a break in the production of manuscripts in the thirteenth century following the Anglo-Norman invasion, the fourteenth century saw a revival of the old manuscript tradition of the eleventh and twelfth centuries. This further continued through the fifteenth and sixteenth centuries and, though being produced in greatly changed circumstances, crucially, this manuscript production, especially legal manuscript production, had the veneer of a tradition unchanged from pre-Norman days. In practice, the situation had changed: not only were Irish society and politics greatly changed, but the very site of production of manuscripts – legal, historical and poetical – had changed, from an exclusively monastic environment to the secular schools of the professional historians, poets and, of most importance to this study, lawyers.

THE IRISH REVIVAL: CHANGES IN THE MANUSCRIPT TRADITION

As Katharine Simms details in *From Kings to Warlords,* the changes which took place in Irish society, politics and warfare after the thirteenth century, variously labelled the Gaelic revival, or even 'renaissance' of the late Middle Ages, exhibited a deliberate choice to re-employ political structures, methods and terminology as they had existed in the eleventh and twelfth centuries. For example secular inauguration rites were revived which had probably fallen into disuse when the English presence in Ireland was at its height. Rather than a continuity between the twelfth century and the fourteenth and fifteenth centuries, this revival indicates a choice on the part of the Irish leadership to revert to these rites.[72] Irish leaders and the learned classes, far from acknowledging this chosen reversion, expressed the choice in terms of a continuity with what was characterised as a vigorous epoch in Irish history.

A similar trend is found in the production of manuscripts. In the period up to the twelfth century, manuscripts were produced almost exclusively in monastic scriptoria in which both Latin and Irish were used.[73] In the eighth and ninth centuries these monasteries suffered greatly from the unrest of the Viking period, which resulted in the destruction of many monastic libraries so that only a fraction of what was written before 850 survived.[74] A change in emphasis is discernible after 900 when the use of Irish comes to predominate over Latin.[75] After the death of Brian Bóramha in 1014 the threat of Norse invasions receded. This, it is said, allowed the eleventh and especially the twelfth century before the Anglo-Norman invasion to be a period of great literary activity.[76] Secular as well as religious material was produced, written in Irish script (whether in the Irish or Latin language) and employing the style of illumination used in the eighth and ninth centuries together with Norse influences.[77]

Although there was much importation of foreign manuscripts in the thirteenth century, there is an almost complete absence of native scribal material. The Gregorian reform and the plunderings of the Anglo-Normans brought about the decline of the old order monasteries. Clerics who took the charge of celibacy seriously left no direct heirs; local ecclesiastical

---

[72] Simms, *From Kings to Warlords*, pp. 16, 29.

[73] Françoise Henry and Geneviève Marsh-Micheli, 'Manuscripts and Illuminations, 1169-1603', in Cosgrove (ed.), *A New History of Ireland II: Medieval Ireland, 1169-1534*, Clarendon Press, Oxford, 1987 p. 783.

[74] John Ryan SJ, 'The Historical Background' in O'Cuiv, *Seven Centuries of Irish Learning 1000-1700*, Published for Radio Eireann by the Stationery Office, 1961 p. 12.

[75] *Ibid.*

[76] For a description see Myles Dillon, 'Literary Activity in the pre-Norman Period', in Seven Centuries of Irish Learning. pp. 27-44.

[77] Henry and Marsh-Micheli, 'Manuscripts and Illuminations', p. 783.

families sometimes found their claim to the bishopric disregarded by a local ruler, who would impose a relative upon the position who usually had no commitment to the traditional learning of the pre-reform monasteries. This pattern was continued after the arrival of the Anglo-Normans by English kings who controlled the appointments of all bishoprics and abbeys, and did not like appointing Irish candidates.[78] The new religious communities of foreign monastic orders that replaced the old order monasteries were chiefly interested in foreign manuscript production methods and styles.[79] The work of these communities thus varies little from that of their contemporaries in England.[80]

The effect of this change on traditional Irish learning is dramatically evidenced by the successive failure of old order monasteries to continue to update their annals. The transfer of this work to hereditary historians, poets and jurists working under the patronage of secular rulers did not occur immediately.[81] By the fourteenth century the site of manuscript production had radically altered. When the old order monasteries closed down they left behind them extensive libraries in which the foreign orders and the Anglo-Normans were not interested. However, in the fourteenth century we find the books of the libraries being studied, copied and adapted by members of secular learned families. These families worked under the patronage of various local rulers, both Irish and the increasingly hibernicised Anglo-Irish.[82] Manuscripts were thus being produced in a very different environment to that of the twelfth century. The remarkable feature of this change, however, was that these secular learned families produced manuscripts in a style identical to that of the great collections of the monastery-centred twelfth century.[83] James Carney notes, for example, that the earliest preserved manuscripts of the fourteenth-century scribe Adhamh O Cianáin, who had access to important twelfth-century manuscripts, appear to be self-consciously imitating a script with which he is not familiar; it becomes natural in style only in later manuscripts.[84] The

---

[78] Katharine Simms, 'The brehons of later medieval Ireland', in Daire Hogan and W.N. Osborough (eds.), *Brehons, Serjeants and Attorneys: Studies in the History of the Irish Legal Profession*, Irish Academic Press, 1990 p. 56.

[79] Henry and Marsh-Micheli, 'Manuscripts and Illuminations', p. 783.

[80] *Ibid.*

[81] Simms, 'The brehons of later medieval Ireland', p. 57.

[82] Henry and Marsh-Micheli, 'Manuscripts and Illuminations', p. 784.

[83] *Ibid.*

[84] Francis John Byrne, 'Introduction', in *The Irish Hand*, p. xxiv.

great changes visible by the fourteenth century obviously must be accounted for in the thirteenth century, but it should be remembered that it is nothing more than the lack of manuscript evidence which gives the impression of a dramatic change.[85] However dramatic or gradual this change was, the important point is that the site of manuscript production had changed, although the manuscripts present the façade of a continuous tradition.

THE RISE OF THE SECULAR LEARNED FAMILIES

This change from a monastic to a secular environment of compilation and composition is associated with the rise to scholarly pre-eminence of the hereditary learned families and has its roots as far back as the tenth century.[86] The annals give an indication of the rise of certain families with the association of particular positions with specific families becoming more noticeable in the twelfth century.[87] Even as early as the twelfth century, heads of these families held high positions. Nevertheless in the twelfth century it is generally difficult to determine whether lay or ecclesiastical status pertains to a historian or a Brehon, making it unclear as to when change from a monastic to secular environment of manuscript production really took place.[88] However, it is clear that by the time of the Gregorian reform and the Anglo-Norman invasion, hereditary families of poets, historians and jurists were attached to powerful rulers, by way of patronage of their schools or in the role of the increasing numbers of professional servitors of these rulers. The learned classes were thus ready to exploit the changed circumstances and absorb the learning and traditions which had been the preserve of the now redundant old order monasteries.[89] It is with the hereditary families of jurists that this study will most concern itself.

---

[85] Henry and Marsh-Micheli, 'Manuscripts and Illuminations', p. 792.

[86] *Ibid.*, p. 790.

[87] *Ibid.* The authors give the example of a family in Connacht which supplies the chief poet of Connacht for long periods and reappears after a period of disfavour.

[88] *Ibid.*, p. 791. Take for example the brehon Ua Duilendáin, 'erenach of Easdara, ollamh of law and chief of his territory', (A.F.M. 1158).

[89] *Ibid.*, p. 792. Hereditary legal families were also found in Wales and Scotland. R.R. Davies, 'The Administration of Law in Medieval Wales', p. 264.

LAW SCHOOLS IN CLASSICAL IRELAND

Law manuscripts were produced in law schools in Ireland at least as early as the seventh century. The canonical texts found in the Irish law manuscripts are a mixture of church and lay subject matter and were written, it seems, in a context where clerics, lay scholars and secular jurists co-operated.[90] Binchy is of the opinion that there were two different law schools when the law texts were first composed, which he refers to as the *Senchas Már* school and the *Bretha Nemed* school.[91] The former, he says, was comprised of professional jurists, while the latter was a poetico-legal school. Both terms cover a range of legal texts written in these different law schools.[92] Evidence from the law texts indicates that the different law schools operated in different areas of Ireland: the *Senchas Már* school or schools may have been somewhere in the Northern midlands.[93] The 'poetico-legal' texts from the *Bretha Nemed* school and other texts such as *Críth Gablach,* which do not seem to have come from either of the first two schools, have a very different approach to legal composition.[94] As one would expect from a situation like this, such things as the amount of a fine for an offence vary among them. This is revealed when, in the later Middle Ages, all the ancient texts are treated as equally valid sources for legal maxims by the secular law schools.[95]

Fergus Kelly in *A Guide to Early Irish Law*[96] says that it is reasonable to assume that there were several centres for legal learning, although there is no real evidence to determine their exact location before the ninth century, when the monasteries of Cloyne, Cork and Slayne are mentioned as legal centres. It is significant that the only places mentioned as centres of legal learning are monasteries, given the change to a secular

---

[90] Liam Breatnach, 'Lawyers in early Ireland', in Daire Hogan and W.N. Osborough (eds.), *Brehons, Serjeants and Attorneys: Studies in the History of the Irish Legal Profession*, Irish Academic Press, 1990 p. 5.

[91] D.A. Binchy, 'Bretha Nemed', *Eriu*, XVII (1955) p. 4.

[92] *Ibid.*, p. 5.

[93] Kelly, *A Guide to Early Irish Law*, p. 242.

[94] *Ibid.*, p. 246.

[95] Kelly notes that a later commentator at CIH 2121.27-9 distinguishes what the fine for a particular offence is in *Crith Gablach,* the *Senchas* and the *Cáin Fuithirbe,* and that the *Crith Gablach* was obviously known to the author of the *Bretha Nemed Toísech* as he refers to its discussion of its lay grades. *Ibid.*, p. 246.

[96] *Ibid.*, p. 242.

environment after the thirteenth century.[97] As to annalistic references to the law schools, Kelly comments that there is no reference to them during the period of composition of the canonical law tracts.[98] Between the ninth and twelfth centuries there are fifteen judges mentioned, but all but four seem to have held high ecclesiastical office.[99] Despite the obvious ecclesiastic involvement, the relationship between Irish law and Canon law is still unclear.[100] Donnchadh O'Corráin has suggested that, owing to the obvious interdependence between the secular tracts and the Canon laws of early Christian Ireland, it may be possible to show that the practitioners of each had effectively merged and formed one profession.[101] Besides the evidence provided by the law tracts of clerical involvement in secular law, there are many references in the annals of the eleventh and twelfth centuries showing that many important ecclesiastics were actually called by the formal title of *an brethem* (the judge).[102] Also, the only pre-fourteenth century law manuscript is probably ecclesiastical in its source.[103]

The hereditary learned families, later to dominate Irish law, began to achieve certain prominence as far back as the tenth century although it is difficult to distinguish whether a judge is lay or ecclesiastic.[104] These jurists, like the clerics, poets and historians, derived from the politically unsuccessful branches of the increasingly powerful ruling families. Thus at this early stage the important link between the ruling families and the

---

[97] Breatnach, 'Lawyers in early Ireland', p. 5.

[98] Kelly, *A Guide to Early Irish Law*, p. 248.

[99] *Ibid.*, p. 249.

[100] Simms, 'The brehons of later medieval Ireland', p. 51. Katharine Simms demonstrates that the church reforms of Canon law at this time resulted in a conflict between long established practices of the Irish church and the less flexible new Canon law system. This would explain why the reforming synods legislated on clerical celibacy and incest yet failed to legislate on the question of Irish marriage, divorce and concubinage practices when such legislation was being made in Europe. This would be natural if laws of marriage were seen as part of the secular law, which was now separate from the church law, the reform of which was the sole preoccupation of the synods. p. 53-54.

[101] Cited in Simms, *Ibid.*, p. 51.

[102] *Ibid.*

[103] Mac Niocaill, 'Aspects of Irish Law in the Late Thirteenth Century', p. 29. This is the Bodleian Library Manuscript, Rawlinson B502.

[104] Henry and Marsh-Micheli, 'Manuscripts and Illuminations,' pp.790-791. Take for example the brehon Ua Duilendáin, 'erenach of Easdara, ollamh of law and chief of his territory', (A.F.M. 1158).

learned classes can be seen.[105] Consistent with the period of transition from a monastic to a secular site for manuscript production, is the silence in the annals between 1232 and 1309, when no brehons are named. Tiobraide O Braoin, whose death is recorded in 1232 was the last distinguished representative of an important ecclesiastical family and was learned in theology, history and law.[106] When the next entry for a lawyer occurs the situation has obviously changed: in 1309 the death of a Mac Aodhagáin (Mac Egan) brehon is recorded.[107]

THE SECULAR LAW SCHOOLS

The Mac Aodhagáin Family

Prior to 1309, it seems the Mac Aodhagáin family were subordinate to the O'Ceallaigh chiefs of East Co. Galway.[108] Throughout the thirteenth century they are recorded as warriors.[109] It is not until the death of Giolla na Naomh Mac Aodhagáin 'ollam of Connacht in law', in 1309, that the Mac Aodhagáin family is connected with law. The annals record that distant cousins of Giolla's died in 1316 and 1320. The recording of these deaths led Katharine Simms to conclude that law may have been studied in the family for some generations before 1309 despite the silence of the annals.[110] Throughout the fourteenth, fifteenth and sixteenth centuries, the Mac Aodhagáins were the principal legal family in Ireland, and most scribes and law manuscripts are somehow connected with their various branches. These branches in turn were strongly connected with ruling families in Connacht and Munster.[111] A branch of the Mac Aodhagáins

---

[105] O'Corráin, 'Nationality and Kingship', p. 18.

[106] Simms, 'The brehons of later medieval Ireland', p. 57.

[107] *Ibid.*, p. 57.

[108] *Ibid.*, p. 58; Mac Niocaill, 'Aspects of Irish Law in the Late Thirteenth Century', p. 29.

[109] Simms, 'The brehons of later medieval Ireland', p. 58.

[110] *Ibid.*, p. 59. See also Mac Niocaill, 'Aspects of Irish Law in the Late Thirteenth Century', p. 29 who also sees the turn to law having occurred several generations earlier.

[111] Henry and Marsh-Micheli, 'Manuscripts and Illuminations', p. 793.

held a law school in Park castle, about twelve miles from Tuam and six from Glenamaddy.[112]

The Mac Aodhagáins were brehons to the McCarthys in Munster, and to the O'Connors in Connacht.[113] In the time of the Irish revival when many Anglo-Irish lords adopted Irish laws as well as customs and speech, they became Brehons to the Burkes of Clanricard and the Barretts of Tyrawley.[114] The Ormond branch of the Mac Aodhagáins was prominent in the fifteenth and sixteenth centuries, with residences in the castle of Annameadle (or Aghnamadle) near Toomavara, BallyMacAodhagáin and Coilte Ruadh, Co. Tipperary.[115] Their most famous law school in Co. Galway was in Duniry near Portumna.[116] It is clear from this brief survey that the Mac Aodhagáins were closely associated with local ruling families.

The oldest manuscript written in their hand is a fragment of the *Senchas Már,* which on the evidence of a dated inscription must pre-date 1350.[117] Of great significance is the fact that the decorative traditions follow those found in the twelfth-century Rawlinson MS B502 manuscript.[118] The Mac Aodhagáins made much use of old manuscripts kept in the old monasteries, and much of their work in this period can be seen to derive from them.[119]

Other legal families

The origins of other legal families such as the Mac Fhlannchadha (Mac Clancy) of Munster and the O Deoradháin (O'Doran) of Leinster are less clear. The O Breisléin (O'Breslin) brehons of Fermanagh, who, like the Mac Aodhagáins, are first recorded in the fourteenth century, were

---

[112] Thomas B. Costello, 'The Ancient Law School of Park, Co. Galway,' *Journal of the Galway Archeological and Historical Society*, 1912 p. 89. The castle is now a ruin.

[113] *Ibid.*

[114] Martin J. Blake, 'Two Irish Brehon scripts: with notes on the MacEgan family', *Journal of the Galway Archeological and Historical Society*, 6 (1909) p. 4.

[115] *Ibid.*, p. 5.

[116] Costello, 'The Ancient Law School', p. 89.

[117] Henry and Marsh-Micheli, 'Manuscripts and Illuminations', p. 796. The inscription is by Aodh, son of Conchobhar Mac Aodhagáin, dated 1350. In it he says he is writing in his father's book.

[118] *Ibid.*, p. 796.

[119] *Ibid.*, p. 796-97.

hereditary church tenants. Brehons as with members of all learned classes, were, it seems, recruited from church tenants, minor nobility and pre-Norman professionals.[120] Another family, the Ua Duibhdabhoireanns (O'Davorens), held a law school in the ancient fort of Cahermacnaghten in the Burren, Co. Clare. It appears to have been first established in 1500 by Giolla na Naomh Mór (son of Aodh, son of Maghnus) Ua Duibhdabhoireann,[121] although the family seems to have been hereditary brehons since the fourteenth century. The earliest reference to the Ua Duibhdabhoireanns as the hereditary brehons to the O'Loghlens is in AFM 1364, where the death of 'Giolla na Naomh Ua Duibhdabhoireann, ollamh of Corcumdhruadh in Brehon law' is recorded.[122] The family was never big like the Mac Aodhagáins, and did not own much land.[123]

It appears that there was much interchange of ideas, and manuscripts for copying, between the different law schools. The Mac Aodhagáin law school in Park seems to have been at the centre of much of this activity, and many comments in the margins of Ua Duibhdabhoireann manuscripts refer to the scribe's temporary presence in Park. Scribes in various manuscripts mention being at Park, Tuam, Rosmanagher, Garranes, Dysartlawrence,[124] Achamaw and Castle Fleming amongst others.[125]

INCREASE IN THE GEOGRAPHICAL AND POLITICAL AREA ADMINISTERED BY IRISH LAW

At the same time as the revival of the manuscript tradition and the rise of the secular legal families, the geographical and political area over which Irish law had jurisdiction expanded. In the first hundred years after the coming of the Anglo-Normans to Ireland (the period in which the colony reached its greatest extent), the English common law supplanted Irish law in many areas of the country. In English-controlled areas Irish law was not allowed to continue and Irish people in these areas were denied access to

---

[120] Simms, 'The brehons of later medieval Ireland', p. 60.

[121] George U. Macnamara, 'The O'Davorens of Cahermachnaughten, Burren, Co. Clare', *North Munster Archeological Society Journal*, 2 (1912-1913), p. 65.

[122] *Ibid.*, p. 77.

[123] *Ibid.*

[124] O'Grady, *Catalogue of Irish Manuscripts*, pp. (Park) 108, 111, 112, 121, (Tuam) 125, 129, 140, (Garranes) 80, (Dysartlawrence) 147.

[125] Abbott & Gwynn, *Catalogue of Manuscripts*, Library of Trinity College, Dublin, p. 348.

the common law. While this represented little change for those formerly unfree under Irish law, those of the formerly free classes found themselves without any legal status and consequently without legal rights.[126] Access to the common law by an Irish person could only be secured by an individual grant of legal status on the condition that the recipient took up civilised English ways. This meant that he could not wear long hair or a moustache, that he could not use the Irish language or dress in Irish clothes, and that he had to adopt an English surname.

But Irish rule was never entirely suppressed. There remained areas not directly affected by English rule where Irish rule continued.[127] The practice and development of Irish law, although affected by the transition from a monastic to a secular environment for production, also continued in some areas.[128] And by the end of the thirteenth century, the political situation had changed again and Irish rulers were once more beginning to assert themselves.[129] Politics, power and military strength were increasingly inseparable after the thirteenth century and profound changes in military organisation and methods took place throughout the period of the fourteenth to the sixteenth centuries. Lordships were established which relied on military strength rather than social obligation for political power,[130] and those with the greatest military strength – even new families – were able to rise to the top.[131] Because leaders could no longer rely on traditional social obligations to raise an army, the raising of private armies became the norm.[132] This assertion of military strength, aided by the use of mercenaries, meant that the Irish armies were able to reoccupy formerly colonised lands.[133]

As the political and military fortunes of the Irish increased, the application and extent of English law declined. In 1316 a petition was sent to England which claimed that fines were being accepted for all felonies, even for the death of Englishmen.[134] This was an adoption of the provision

---

[126] For the status of the native Irish at common law see: G.J. Hand, *English Law in Ireland 1290-1324,* Cambridge University Press, London. 1967.

[127] Richter, *Medieval Ireland*, p. 151.

[128] *Ibid.*

[129] *Ibid.*, p. 154.

[130] Richter, *Medieval Ireland*, p. 169.

[131] *Ibid.*

[132] *Ibid.*, p. 183.

[133] Simms, *From Kings to Warlords*, p. 18.

[134] Hand, *English Law in Ireland 1290-1324*, p. 208.

in Irish law for an *eraic*-fine for felonies. Similarly, in the 1350s the cities of Ireland presented a petition to the justiciar condemning the lack of English law in the shires and the common occurrence of the issuing of pardons to felons. This was in contrast, they claimed, to what they characterised as the previous situation when the colony was at its height, where judges frequently visited the counties, and felons were hanged.[135] It was not until the 23 Ordinances for Ireland were promulgated in 1331 that a general extension of English law to the Irish was granted. In theory this should have meant that the old racial distinction was to be largely ignored; it seems however that this action was too late. Twenty years later the Statutes of Kilkenny had to forbid the use of the Brehon Law by the Anglo-Irish.[136] Such was the recovery of the native law that even the Anglo-Irish were using it.

As the application of English common law and English control generally declined, the Anglo-Irish increasingly adopted Irish law: in the fourteenth century the 'White' Earl of Ormond had Irish Brehons (the Mac Fhlannchadhas and probably also the Mac Craiths) in his service administering justice in his Earldom. James Butler (the son of the White Earl's nephew Edmond), enacted his 'Acts of Kilcash' in 1478 in which a purely Gaelic system of criminal law is embodied.[137] The Anglo-Irish, like the Irish, treated their illegitimate children in the same way as their legitimate. Under Irish law they had a full right to inherit, even though under English law they were denied any such rights.[138] The Anglo-Irish also adopted Irish marriage practices from this time on.[139] Curtis says:

> The Anglo Irish adopted Brehon law, partly of necessity, partly because their subjects had an invincible attachment to it, partly because the profits were so great and besides, their own origins dated back to a time when feudal, Celtic, and Germanic law had nothing repugnant for one another. Everywhere in the sixteenth century the Tudor officials found the 'degenerate English' using Brehon law. Even Sir Piers Roe had an Irish brehon over his country – Rory MacLaughire.[140]

---

[135] Robin Frame, *English Lordship in Ireland 1318-1361*, Clarendon Press, Oxford, 1982 p. 4.

[136] Hand, *English Law in Ireland 1290-1324*, p. 210.

[137] K.W. Nicholls, 'Anglo-French Ireland and After', *Peritia*, 1 (1982) , p. 401.

[138] Richter, *Medieval Ireland*, p. 170.

[139] *Ibid.*, p. 182.

[140] E. Curtis, *A History of Medieval Ireland from 1086-1513,* (2nd Edn.), Methuen, London, 1938 p. 369.

And so not only was there a change in the sites of legal manuscript production evident from the fourteenth century onward, but also a change in the area over which Irish law had jurisdiction. Although never regaining the unrivalled position it had held in pre-Norman days,[141] the re-establishment of Irish kingship involved also the re-establishment of Irish law over much of the country.

CONCLUSION

What then does this contribute to our discussion of the later juristic scribal activity? It seems we are presented with a paradox. On one hand we have seen the great changes which are taking place in Irish society in this period, particularly following the decline of the colony and the Irish revival. Crucially, the geographical area over which Irish law (in whatever form it took) had jurisdiction increased substantially, with both the recovery of control by Irish leaders and also the adoption of Irish law by some of the Anglo-Irish. On the other hand, the picture of Irish law that we are given by the manuscripts of this time is, allegedly, one of a continuous legal tradition which is immutable and unchanged from earlier times. Like the production of manuscripts of the other traditions and the revival of some twelfth-century rites (particularly of inauguration), they followed twelfth-century styles and used twelfth-century material. Such a situation is striking, given that the manuscripts are being produced in a radically different immediate environment and in a radically different political situation to those that were produced in the twelfth century.

It is clear that the legal tradition was not continuous, if only because it had to re-establish itself in many areas. The received view is to see the manuscripts produced by this legal tradition as stationary against a shifting background. But the relationship between the manuscript and its 'background' is necessarily relative because this background is, of course, composed of nothing more than a variety of other texts which have survived from the period. It is the great tension in the law manuscripts, between stasis and change, (lacking in the texts of the period that seem more sensitive to widespread social change) which makes the law manuscripts so fascinating, and which I will go on to examine. That the study of these texts was deliberately, and improbably, continued in a very changed environment suggests, I would argue, a great deal more than a mere engagement with the past for the past's sake.

---

[141] Particularly with the operation of separate schools of Canon law.

III. LEGAL INTERPRETATION

This is the Cain Patraic and no human Brehon of the Gaedhil is able to abrogate anything that is found in the Senchas Már.

Prologue to the Senchas Már, AL, Vol 1, p.19 Text.

...our craving for certainty may cause us to search for the immutable. This is most apparent in law, where the myth of certainty has a persistent appeal. But the law cannot be certain, in large part because language itself is not certain.

Frederick Schauer, 'An Essay on Constitutional Language', in Sanford Levinson and Stephen Mailloux (Eds.), *Interpreting Law and Literature: A Hermeneutic Reader*, Northwestern University Press, Evanston, IL, 1988 p.153.

One of the most common criticisms levelled at the late medieval Irish jurists is that they were not only committed to the preservation of antiquated and irrelevant texts, but that they treated the law the texts contained as immutable and unchanged, derived from the wisdom of the ancients. Irish society had changed significantly from the time the law tracts were first composed, and yet they continued to be copied and interpreted even though they apparently accorded little with their society. The received view argues that this demonstrates the antiquarianism and excessive conservatism of the later jurists. In this chapter I will be arguing that, contrary to this view, the jurists were using an established way of keeping their texts alive in the present. I wish to look closely at the use of interpretation; in particular I will be examining the methods of glossing and commenting, and the approach to interpretation this implies.

INTERPRETING 'FIXED' TEXTS

According to Mazzeo[142] there exist in every culture texts which are intrinsically important to the knowledge system and value structure of that culture. Here 'texts' are taken in a broad sense and not just in a written

---

[142] Joseph Mazzeo, *Varieties of Interpretation*, University of Notre Dame Press, Notre Dame, 1978 p. vii.

form. Their importance is such that these texts must remain 'fixed'; yet while these texts are theoretically immutable, the social and cultural context in which they are interpreted necessarily changes. The texts thus come, through time, to exist in a different social and political context. This change in context may make an understanding of the texts more difficult, resulting in the 'apparent' meaning of the texts contradicting contemporary knowledge and values. There exists then a conflict between the need to retain the intrinsically important texts, and the peculiar demands of the contemporary cultural context. It is the process of interpretation which seeks to resolve this conflict. As Mazzeo argues;

> ...the interpreter mediates and slows down the processes of cultural change by recreating meaning.[143]

It is in precisely this sort of re-creation of meaning that I would argue the Irish jurists were engaged. At this point, in order to clarify the way in which modern, general interpretative theory may be applied to legal manuscripts, it may be useful to examine the theory of textual interpretation in a modern but specifically legal context.

EXCURSUS: INTERPRETING THE AUSTRALIAN CONSTITUTION

The Australian Constitution was proclaimed on January 1, 1901 when the Australian states formed a federation. It embodies a mixture of the theories and structures of the Westminster system and the United States Constitution. As a document, the entire Australian legal system requires that it be definitive as to how the Commonwealth government is to operate, and how the Federation is to work. Despite its written nature, the Australian Constitution relies heavily on convention and interpretation for its implementation – for example, it is only by convention that Australia has a prime minister. If the words of the Constitution were to be taken literally the Queen's representative, the Governor General, would be a virtual dictator. He would merely be advised by his appointed ministers and would, as constitutional Chief of the Armed Forces, be able to declare war. That this is not the case, and that by convention the Governor General is merely a legal figurehead, is fairly clear.[144]

---

[143] *Ibid.,* p. x.

[144] Although there is still much debate about the exact nature of the convention following the actions of the Governor General in the 1975 Constitutional crisis.

This is a situation analogous, in many ways, with the arguments for the antiquarianism of the later Irish jurists. If a person entirely unacquainted with Australia and its political and legal conventions were to compare the Australian Constitution with political and legal realities since Federation, they might come to a similar conclusion: here is a society whose legal and political élite in particular is committed to preserving a document which does not realistically represent the system of government.

The Australian Constitution is a document intrinsically important to Australia, and it is imperative to the continuance of the Australian Federation that the Constitution be retained. No person or parliament may change any of the words of which it consists, because it is 'fixed' by a rule requiring a referendum of a majority of people in a majority of states to give their approval to amendments. Such a requirement has been notoriously difficult to fulfil, a difficulty which has become so apparent that another imperative has presented itself: that the changes of the past century be accommodated by the Constitution if it is realistically to continue. Owing to the enormous social and cultural changes which have taken place since the 1890s when it was drafted, the Constitution now exists, without any doubt, in a very changed context to that within which it was drafted.

The means to a resolution of these two opposing imperatives has been interpretation. It is because of judicial interpretation that the Constitution has not remained static. The Constitution confers a power for the establishment of a High Court of Australia with the exclusive jurisdiction to interpret the Constitution. Far from being mechanical, such interpretation has been the source of great change. As the gap between the time in which the document was written and the present becomes greater, the more important becomes the bridge of interpretation. While the method by which this interpretation has proceeded has varied (form versus substance, the intention of the Fathers of Federation versus the words in their present context etc.) the fact remains that 'meaning' has changed. So much so that the present interpretation of some sections would be unrecognisable to the writers of those sections, just as much as today's world at large would be unrecognisable.[145] The process of interpretation is the means by which the words of the past may be given effect in the present, in which a culturally significant text may be preserved and yet

---

[145] Changes have followed a greater concentration of power in the Commonwealth over the states, an appreciation of Australia's role in the world at large, a concern for the environment, and the increasingly complex nature of trade, commerce and technology amongst other things.

remain relevant in a changed cultural and social context. An old text may only remain viable in the present through interpretation.

LEGAL FICTIONS

The process of interpretation is complex. In a legal context what is important is how a system characterises this process. Although I have suggested that interpretation allows for change of that which is 'fixed', a legal system will not generally admit such scope, for if a text is to be called 'fixed' it must appear unchanged. What begins to emerge is the importance of fiction in the preservation of 'fixed' texts. Some form of fiction is probably present in any form of interpretation but not all interpretation requires, as that of a 'fixed' text does, that the 'original' meaning of the text be strictly maintained. What makes the interpretation of 'fixed' texts so much more fascinating is that their interpretation is elusive and highly misleading in its nature: it relies on and promotes fictions which conceal the change it achieves. In a sense it is radicalism masked by conservatism. For a text may only retain its 'canonical' form, and at the same time continue to be a living force in the present, through the use of fictions. The choice becomes one of whether to adapt a text to the present through interpretation based on fictions, thereby preserving it, or to abandon it. There is no third way: a text cannot continue to be relevant and yet retain its 'letter' without interpretation founded on fictions. As Mazzeo puts it;

> ...interpretation saves the necessary fiction and domesticates it.[146]

A text which is not interpreted for the present cannot continue to survive.

A system of law based on the written word and almost inevitably relying heavily on 'fixed' texts is, probably more than in other fields, inherently prone to the use of fictions or what we might call 'legal fictions'. A legal fiction, according to Maine, is:

> ...[a]ny assumption which conceals, or effects to conceal, the fact that a rule of law has undergone alteration, its letter remaining unchanged, its operation being modified.[147]

---

[146] Mazzeo, Varieties of Interpretation, p. 115.

[147] Sir Henry Sumner Maine, *Ancient Law: Its connection with the early history of society and its relation to modern ideas,* Oxford University Press, London, 1861 (1954 reprint), p.22. Cited also in most legal dictionaries. See for example John

The Western legal systems abound in legal fictions on varying levels, but perhaps the most significant of these is the fiction of the unchanging meaning of a text. The interpretation of the Australian Constitution is only one example of the use of this widespread fiction. The English common law system has traditionally operated under several basic fictions which deny that change in meaning is achieved through interpretation. There is an answer to any legal problem, according to one fiction, and this answer is expressed in the form of a rule which may be found in a previous authoritative judgment. If it is not to be found there, it may be 'discovered' by a judge because the law 'resides in the breasts of the judges'. Even in the seemingly mystical process of discovery, the application of the law is merely mechanical: the judge applies law which already exists, he does not make it or invent it. The law is thus said to be certain, objectively determinable and applicable and interpretation merely explains and describes that which already has separate existence. The English common law system is also declared to be based on a continuous and unbroken tradition. A law enacted or developed in the Middle Ages, if not repealed by Parliament, is still, in theory, identically applicable today. The law does not change: in its own eyes, a changed cultural and social context makes no difference to its 'fixed' meaning.

The interpretative activity of the late medieval Irish jurists rested upon comparable and historically linked fictions. These are identified by Binchy where he holds that they regarded their texts as immutable, unified and consistent, and as continuous and unchanged from the times of the ancients.[148] Like the fictions of the English common law, fictions surrounded the Irish law manuscripts, that the canonical texts could validly be applied in a changed cultural context, and that this application was merely mechanical. In the Irish law manuscripts we find many explicit statements which seek to promote such fictions. There are many statements contained in both text and gloss that emphasise the immutability of the ancient law. For example in the prologue to the *Senchas Már,* cited at the beginning of this chapter:

> This is the Cain Patraic and no human Brehon of the Gaedhil is able to abrogate anything that is found in the *Senchus Mor*.[149]

Burke, *Osborn's Concise Law Dictionary*, 6th Ed., Sweet and Maxwell, London, 1976 under 'fiction, legal'.

[148] Binchy, 'Ancient Irish Law', p. 88-89.

[149] AL, Vol I, p. 19. Text.

LINKS WITH LATE MEDIEVAL ROMAN AND CANON LAW

In the Irish law manuscripts interpretation occurs through the techniques of gloss and commentary. Interpretation of the Bible and late medieval Roman and Canon law also used a similar method of exegesis through gloss and commentary. Thus the method of exegesis used in later Irish legal manuscripts was neither unusual nor individual to Ireland. The exegetical technique of transcribing the ancient authoritative text in large letters, then to be surrounded and explained by gloss and expanded upon with secondary commentary, was first used in the interpretation of the Bible. After the eleventh century, when there was a revival of the study of Justinian's code in Europe, the techniques of glossing and later of commenting were applied to these texts. These methods were also used in the interpretation of ecclesiastical law which derived much from the newly revived and interpreted Roman law.

Not only was the Irish technique remarkably similar to the Biblical and late medieval Roman and Canon law techniques, but it seems distinctly likely to have been directly influenced by them. Irish law texts were first glossed in the eighth century. As we saw in the second chapter, this glossing would have taken place in an ecclesiastical setting, and the influence of the Biblical technique is not difficult to assume. Timothy O'Neill states that the technique of glossing was first derived from the grammar teachers in the monastic schools.[150] The influence of late medieval Canon law and Roman law is further likely as secular law students in the late medieval period could also attend schools which taught the Canon and Roman law. There are, for instance, references in the annals throughout the late medieval period to jurists trained in both native and Canon or Roman law. Also, the later legal writing demonstrates that later medieval commentators clearly had a knowledge of Canon law. Commentaries occasionally contain citations from Canon law, often side by side with citations from Old Irish law tracts, apparently, it is said, awarding equal validity to both.[151]

INTERPRETATIVE FICTIONS AND EXEGETICAL METHODS

Peter Goodrich, an English legal theorist, argues that the exegetical technique used on the Bible and Canon and Roman law was intricately

---

[150] O'Neill, *The Irish Hand*, p. 32.
[151] Simms, 'The brehons of later medieval Ireland', p. 70.

connected with the legal fictions that their authoritative interpretation relied upon.

> That meaning came to be conceived by the exegetical tradition as given or monologic implies that it has a source, an authority or singular authorship that originally sets out the meaning and whose 'will' may be analytically or exegetically recovered.[152]

He argues that the Bible was held to be a sacred text and, according to the Christian church, each word and letter was authoritative in that it could reveal the will of God. The authority of the text lay in its source.[153] Exegesis on the text was to discover or retrieve what the 'true' will of God was. Similarly, Justinian's code of Roman law, as it was studied in the late medieval European law schools, relied on two basic legal fictions. Firstly, that Roman law as codified by Justinian was 'immediately valid authority', and secondly that society had not changed since the days of Justinian.[154] The result was that there was no need for change in the law because the original meaning could be retrieved and the results of this meaning would adequately meet the needs of the contemporary society. Goodrich says:

> The techniques of legal science developed by the glossators in relation to the Justinian codes were philological in the extreme, they were techniques which presupposed the absolute, Biblical, authority of the texts of the Civil Law.[155]

Glossing on the Irish texts, as we have seen, rested on very similar legal fictions. The jurists held that the law texts derived from the wisdom of the ancients, and because of the authority derived from the texts' antiquity, they were a valid and authoritative source of law. It was through strict exegesis of the texts that the original meaning intended by these ancient authors was to be retrieved.

The interpretative methods in each of these traditions relied also on a legal fiction that the text could be a complete and consistent source of law. This particular legal fiction asserts that the text is thus definitive: all

---

152 Peter Goodrich, 'Law and Language: An Historical and Critical Introduction', p. 177.

153 Peter Goodrich, *Reading the Law: A Critical Introduction to Legal Method and Techniques*, Basil Blackwell Ltd., Oxford, 1986 p. 92.

154 Julian H. Franklin, *Jean Bodin and the Sixteenth Century Revolution in the Methodology of Law and History*, London, 1963 p. 9. Franklin attributes this to a lack of historical perspective on the part of the glossators.

155 Goodrich, 'Law and Language,' p. 177.

answers to legal problems are contained in the text and recourse need not be had outside the text. The legal fiction implies that, by careful exegesis, it is always possible to extend the rules in the text to new situations by interpreting through analogies, similarities and deductions. This further assumes that there is uniformity or unity of meaning within the text and that the code should not be criticised if contradictions appear. If such contradictions occur the proper technique is rather to search for the true meaning of the words and thereby reconcile contradictions.[156] Thus, not only is exegesis to find the 'true' and 'original' meaning of words or 'rules', but it must be confined to the text and must systematise that which contains incompatibilities. Of late Roman law, Franklin says:

> It was assumed...that the *Corpus Juris,* by and large, was a self-contained and internally consistent whole, the rules of which were valid universally. And the method of interpretation was internal logical analysis.[157]

One of the apparently defective features of the glosses and commentaries on the Irish law texts is the similar attempt to reconcile inconsistencies between different texts. As we saw earlier, it seems likely that the canonical texts of the seventh and eighth centuries were written in different parts of Ireland at different times, and so are divergent in their treatment of some matters. However, as the later medieval jurists treated them all as equally valid sources of law, they tried to harmonise the differences between them. This they did in a way reminiscent of late medieval Roman law, of which Franklin says:

> The great majority [of the glosses]...are interpretations of a word or passage, the sense of which was normally suggested to the glossator by his knowledge of related passages in other portions of the *Corpus.* Indeed, there are many glosses in which this process of internal comparison is made explicit, in the form of citations to related passages. And when one such passage is in apparent conflict with another, a distinction was sometimes offered to resolve the contradiction.[158]

ESTABLISHING THE AUTHORITY OF THE TEXT

As we have said, the very technique of glossing and commenting on the earlier law texts was intimately connected with the legal fictions upon

---

[156] Goodrich, *Reading the Law*, p. 94.

[157] Franklin, *Jean Bodin*, p. 9.

[158] *Ibid.*, p. 9-10.

which the interpretation of these texts relied. The bases of these legal fictions are formalist beliefs in the rule of law and the mechanical role for legal interpretation. Goodrich argues that the authoritative status of the Bible came not so much from the text itself (which is what its interpreters claimed) but from the way in which the text was treated.[159] He argues that the process of glossing and commenting on a primary text was a way of establishing the importance and authority of that text.[160] Binchy says that the copious glossing and commenting on the *Senchas Már* was largely worthless in interpreting the Old Irish text. However, it does seem that the presence of such a rich apparatus of gloss and commentary was important in establishing the *Senchas Már* as the principal text for study and application. Other texts, which appear to have been copied and studied less assiduously, lacked this kind of apparatus. *Críth Gablach*, for example, of which only three manuscript witnesses survive (none of them complete), is almost devoid of glosses and commentary.

The interpretative techniques of glossing and commenting are important to give authority to the principle text. Thus it is not just that the text is authoritative and so receives attention, but that the attention it receives is crucial to actually establish its authority. Goodrich argues that glossing and commenting was also a technique of commenting on and controlling the meaning of the text.[161] By interpreting and making old texts relevant to the present, glossing and commenting promotes the idea that the text can offer solutions to all legal problems and that the law is unchanged and unchangeable. The text must be made compatible because it is on its authority that all legal decisions must be based.[162] And yet, of course, this requires adherence to the fiction that interpretation does not change the law, but merely explicates it – that there is an objectively determinable meaning capable of being applied in the same way, over time and regardless of time.

ADAPTING IMMUTABLE LAW TO CHANGED CIRCUMSTANCES

The law in its written form is not perfect or consistent, and must be subject to change. Law must adapt to society in order to remain alive and authoritative. And yet, as we have seen, to remain authoritative it must

---

[159] Goodrich, *Reading the Law*, p. 93.
[160] *Ibid.*, p. 93.
[161] *Ibid.*
[162] *Ibid.*, p. 99-100.

also stress that it does not change, that its meanings are fixed and that interpretation merely recovers these meanings. It is, however, through the marriage of method and fiction that the tension between stasis and change seeks to resolve itself.

The development and expansion of the import and scope of earlier legal terminology has often been the only way in which a law based on fixed texts could change without legislation by an authoritative person or body. As we saw in the example of the Australian Constitution, this is typically the only practical way that changes in a written constitution may be achieved. Similarly, in the Irish legal system it has been argued convincingly that 'there was no person or institution authorised openly to change the law'[163] and so one might conclude that the importance of this practice was even more pronounced in that historical context. It may well be that:

> Irish law...was hamstrung by its adherence to a collection of canonical texts of the seventh–eighth centuries, and the study and practice of law were the explanation and application of the precepts of these texts. [164]

Yet such an approach does not inevitably lead to the conclusions that Irish law was unable to change and that it lacked any sense of vitality in the later Middle Ages. Perhaps instead of 'hamstrung' we might simply say that Irish law in this period was distinguished by its adherence to canonical texts. And, as we have seen, such an adherence is not anomalous, but is, it may be conjectured, a common element in ancient and modern legal systems.

Thomas says that it was the strength of the Roman law that the work of the glossators allowed for this change.[165] European society had changed since the time of Justinian. The technique of the glossators, however, allowed for change in the meaning of the texts whilst maintaining the legal fictions it was based on. The work of the late medieval Irish jurists may also, I believe, be viewed as a method through which change could occur, and adherence to the letter of the canonical texts could be maintained.

It is said that the later medieval jurists were often explaining legal maxims and terms, the meanings of which they could not always comprehend. The result, so this view declares, was misunderstanding and misapplication of the 'true' meaning of the texts. An example of this

---

[163] Gearoid Mac Niocaill, 'The Interaction of Laws' in James Lydon (ed.), *The English in Medieval Ireland*, Royal Irish Academy, Dublin, 1984 p. 109.

[164] *Ibid.*

[165] J.A.C. Thomas, *Textbook of Roman Law*, Amsterdam, North Holland, 1976 p. 5n.

supposed misunderstanding and misapplication may be found in Binchy's edition of *Coibnes Uisci Thairidne*, a tract that deals with water mills. The text is not glossed by a single scribe: Binchy identifies three different hands in the glosses and commentaries, and shows that in places the different glossators disagree on a point of interpretation.[166] The manuscript of the sole complete copy was written between the fourteenth and sixteenth centuries. The scribe who transcribed the canonical text is unknown. His habit of omitting words has led the glossators to insert emendations in the margins.[167] Most of the glosses were written by Lucas O Dalláin whose script has been found in another fourteenth-century manuscript,[168] but other glosses are added by Aedh Mac Aodhagáin and Caibre (a common name among the Mac Aodhagáins). Because a comment of Aedh is dated Christmas Eve 1550, we know that the work of the unknown scribe and the principal glossator must have been carried out before this date. Caibre occasionally makes additions to the glosses of the other two which, Binchy says, shows him to be the latest of the three.[169] The commentaries were written in the margin by the principal glossator and by Caibre.[170] Binchy says:

> Sometimes they [the glossators] seem merely to be guessing at the meaning of institutions which were obsolete in their day. Take for example their efforts to explain *déolaid* 'gratis' as applied to the shares of the 'source' and the 'pond' in the rotation of the mill. According to L [principal glossator] this means that the owner of the 'source' is dispensed from casting lots with the other partners in order to determine the order of priority between them, whereas A [Aedh] suggests that he is simply freed from the duty of constructing the mill-race, an 'explanation' which L himself had already advanced for *déolaid* in regard to the owner of the 'pond'. Neither interpretation is correct. The true meaning is supplied by an earlier glossator in H 4. 22, p. 20 (O'C 1982) who defines the 'share in the mill' (*cuit i mmuiliunn*) possessed by the partners as *bleith deolaid...cin fochraic do gabail de* 'free grinding...without a fee being taken from him'. In the text, therefore, *déolaid* means exactly what it says, and these later interpretations are quite fanciful.[171]

---

[166] Binchy, 'Irish Law Tracts Re-edited: I. Coibnes Uisci Thairidne', p. 53-54.

[167] *Ibid.*, p. 55.

[168] *Ibid.*, p. 55.

[169] *Ibid.*, p. 55.

[170] *Ibid.*, p. 55.

[171] *Ibid.*, p. 61.

It is arguable that the scholars who propound or subscribe to the received view – that the activity of the late medieval Irish jurists was antiquarian – are, in many ways similar to the late medieval Irish jurists themselves, formalist in their approach to 'meaning'. That is, these scholars assume there is an objective original meaning for any legal term, and the failure of the later jurists to 'accurately' retrieve this is evidence that they misunderstood their texts. However proponents of modern legal theory argue that 'legal meaning' cannot be determined objectively nor will it be immediately apparent; that lawyers are engaged in interpretation of the words formulated as rules. In this, law may be understood as a language based field of study and practice. The assertion that a proper legal decision will give effect to the 'true' or 'original' meaning of a 'legal rule' may be said itself to be a fiction, if, perhaps, a necessary one: for any decision, this theory argues, is an interpretation. If we accept these arguments then we may regard the 'misexplanation' of the jurists as an inevitability of the legal process and legal change through interpretation.

Gearoid Mac Niocaill quotes the English legal historian Maitland as saying:

> A lawyer finds on his table a case about rights of common which sends him to the Statute of Merton. But is it really the law of 1236 that he wants to know? No, it is the ultimate result of the interpretations set on the statute by the judges of twenty generations. That process...is from the lawyer's point of view an evolution of the true intent and meaning of the old law; from the historian's point of view it is almost of necessity a process of perversion and misunderstanding.[172]

Thus legal fictions used in the interpretation of a text required to be 'fixed' – as a statute generally is – allow for flexibility. The historian is not wrong to point to a misunderstanding of the original statute. It is inevitable that the way a law in the language of 1236 was understood then, and the way it is understood now, are, owing to intervening social, cultural and linguistic change, highly different. It is not a process of 'perversion' and 'misunderstanding' but a way of maintaining an important text by allowing for modifications to accommodate social and cultural change. The historian described by Maitland, misunderstands the importance to legal development of the maintenance of the fiction which says that an expanded and modified interpretation of an old law is merely explicating its full and original meaning. It is a way to counter the natural

---

[172] Gearoid Mac Niocaill, 'Notes on Litigation in Late Irish Law', p. 304-5.

conservatism of the law whilst maintaining its authority. The law must change but it must retain its authority.

In reference to the United States Constitution, the words of the American legal theorist, Frederick Schauer, are to the point. Schauer uses the example of the ship imagined by the philosopher Neurath, which is to be rebuilt plank by plank while it is still afloat. He says:

> So long as the ship stays afloat during the process, it is no objection that the finished product bears little or no relation to the original. With Constitutional language, so long as the enterprise stays afloat it is no objection that the current conception bears no close relation to the ordinary language meaning of the text. If we have moved in small steps from the original text, the enterprise stays afloat.[173]

Thus what is vital to the legal system is that the canonical text continues to have authority. To have this authority, it must be continually reinterpreted for the present. And yet this interpretation cannot drastically alter the text. Gradual change, where the end bears little relation to the original, allows authority to be maintained and change to be incorporated.

GLOSSES AND TRANSLATION

The notion of interpretation of earlier legal texts involves also an appreciation of the parallel concept of translation. As I have already said, interpretation, especially of a 'fixed' text, attempts to bridge the gap which occurs between the past and the present as a result of social and cultural changes. This process goes further. Law in a written form is written in a particular language of a particular time. When we come to explain it in another, we must bridge not just social and cultural changes but changes which have occurred in that language itself because language is the most sensitive register of social and cultural change.[174] If we proceed on the basis that, with a 'fixed' text, the words must be given their 'original' meaning this requires that the language be maintained as a distinct one, and the old terms are 'translated' to recast the meaning in new terms. Glossing is thus a form of translation.

The following example demonstrates the method by which the glosses 'translate' old text. For our purposes it is important to observe how

[173] Schauer, 'An Essay on Constiitutional Language', p. 151.
[174] James Boyd White, *Justice as Translation: An Essay in Cultural and Legal Criticism*, University of Chicago Press, Chicago, 1990 p. 240.

the words of the text are 'translated' or recast into different words in the gloss.

> COIBNIUS UISCI THAIRIDNE HI FINTEDAIB GRIAIN AS(AS)A TAIRI[D]NIDER
>
> .i. ata coibintius no comducus don ine isinn uisce tairngithir and a dualgus ind earraind dara tairgit*er* e.
>
> [THERE IS] KINSHIP OF CONDUCTED WATER IN THE KINSHARES OF THE LAND OUT OF WHICH IT IS LED
>
> The family has kinship or joint right of inheritance in the water which is conducted there by right of the land across which it is conducted.[175]

The fiction on which the technique of glossing rests, of course argues that such translation retrieves the 'original meaning' of the old words and merely expresses this meaning in more modern language. However, giving new life to old words in a changed cultural context necessarily entails a loss of old meaning and the gaining of new. James Boyd White says:

> ...in this process of translation there is always gain and always loss, always transformation;...the "original meaning" of the text cannot be our meaning, for in restating it in our terms, in our world, no matter how faithfully or literally, we produce something new and different.[176]

In this way it could be said that there is no translation that is not at the same time an interpretation.

The proposition that glossing on the Irish law texts is an act of translation may be further understood by examining the substantial changes in language that had occurred from the time of the earliest texts. Some legal terms had fallen into disuse and others had taken their place. There was thus a need to make them more readily understandable in the present. The glosses are largely based on a word or phrase in the main text, which they re-explain in more modern terms. In transferring the old meaning into new language (based on the fiction that this is possible without loss or change of meaning), changes in legal meaning with various degrees of obviousness can be observed. This change in meaning occurred

---

[175] Text and translation excerpted from: Binchy, 'Irish Law Tracts Re-edited: I. Coibnes Uisci Thairidne', pp. 64-65. For an alternative translation of the text (not the gloss) see Rolf Baumgarten, 'The Kindred Metaphors in "Bechbretha" and "Coibnes Uisci Thairidne" ', *Peritia*, 4, (1985) p. 318.

[176] White, *Justice as Translation*, p. 241.

particularly where social and political structures had altered. A very clear and unusual example of this is best seen in a late thirteenth-century precis of Irish law written by Giolla na Naomh Mac Aodhagáin, the author of the poem referred to earlier in this work. The text proclaims itself to be a rendering into 'clear Irish' of a difficult Irish 'corpus'.[177] Mac Niocaill acknowledges that the 'mere fact of translation into terms both comprehensible and familiar to a student inevitably permitted more or less contemporary reality to percolate through the text'.[178] The text deals with the law of social obligation and the distinctions made seem naturally to reflect the Irish social structure of the late thirteenth century, although it is at times more conservative on points such as the prerogatives of the king.[179] Although there is, in the thirteenth century, a perceivable appearance of something like the 'king's peace' in England, nevertheless, according to Mac Niocaill, all the rules cited have a basis in the canonical texts.[180]

Another example of change through translation is found in the following gloss:

A COIMDED DO CUMDACH .i. a tigearna do cumdach.

TO PROTECT HIS LORD, i.e. to defend his lord.[181]

This shows the replacement of the term *coimded* (for Old Irish *coimdiu*) with the term which became current in the later Middle Ages, *tigearna*. Such a change is not simply terminological but reflects substantial change in political organisation in Ireland.

A practical use of linguistic change to allow for change of meaning can be seen in the following example from early Biblical exegesis.

In the story of Cain and Abel (Gen. 4), Cain complains to God about the punishment that has been given him for murdering his brother; his words are, "Lo, my punishment is too great to bear." To a later age, however, the word used for "punishment" seemed strange, for it had long since ceased to mean punishment and now meant only sin or crime. Jewish exegetes played on this confusion in order to turn Cain into the figure of a repentant sinner, and instead of having him complain to God that his punishment is too

---

[177] Mac Niocaill, 'Aspects of Irish Law in the Late Thirteenth Century', p. 30. He says it is obviously aimed at the student.

[178] *Ibid.*, p. 31.

[179] *Ibid.*, p. 34.

[180] *Ibid.*, pp. 34-35.

[181] *AL.*, Vol. III, pp. 22- 23.

> severe, Cain is made out to be saying "Lo, my sin is too great to forgive," quite a different sentiment! The reasons for this "interpretation" may have been ideological, but it was founded on a linguistic reality, the perceived strangeness or inappropriateness of the biblical usage to later readers.[182]

Thus, by an apparently innocent explication of an old term in modern terms, and by inadvertently giving the modern meaning to an older word that has changed its meaning, a considerable amount of new life may be generated from old texts. The radical departures from the 'original meaning' of a text, which critics of the later jurists point to, may be seen as very obvious instances of the creation of new life and not 'incomprehension'. Whether or not the later jurists understood the words they were translating is not the point. Binchy, in a discussion on the changing capacity of a married woman to contract, says that the later jurists 'rob' the earlier terminology of its force by interpreting it with extreme restrictiveness.[183] Restrictive or not, the point is that their interpretative activity changes meaning.

COMMENTARY: ESTABLISHING A HIERARCHY OF SECONDARY AUTHORITIES

Translating the language of the Old Laws into a contemporary language was only one way of ensuring the preservation of these 'fixed' texts. Commentary is an even more important method by which the meaning of the old law could change. In the manuscripts the relationship between text and commentary is not as direct as the relationship between text and gloss. Although some commentaries do explicate an earlier tract, in the main, the commentaries were written independently of the old text and then appended to it because of the subject matter.

The Biblical and late medieval Roman and Canon law method of exegesis was based on a primary text to which the exegesis provided a secondary literature in the form of glosses and particularly commentaries. This secondary literature, as we have seen, established that a text had authority – it then provided a secondary hierarchy of authorities according to the order of the commentaries.[184] Maine recognises this same process in

---

[182] James L. Kugel, 'Early Interpretation: The Common Background of Late Forms of Biblical Exegesis', in Kugel and Greer, *Early Biblical Interpretation*, The Westminster Press, Philadelphia, 1986 p.30.

[183] Mac Niocaill, 'Aspects of Irish Law in the Late Thirteenth Century', p. 27.

[184] Goodrich, *Reading the Law*, p. 93.

his commentary on the *Responsa Prudentium* from an earlier period in Roman law. He says:

> The form of these responses varied a good deal at different periods of the Roman jurisprudence, but throughout its whole course they consisted of explanatory glosses on authoritative written documents, and at first they were exclusively collections of opinions interpretative of the Twelve Tables. As with us [English common law system], all legal language adjusted itself to the assumption that the text of the old Code remained unchanged. There was the express rule. It overrode all glosses and comments, and no-one openly admitted that any interpretation of it, however eminent the interpreter, was safe from revision on appeal to the venerable texts. Yet in point of fact, Books of Responses bearing the names of leading juriconsults obtained an authority at least equal to that of our reported cases, and constantly modified, extended, limited, or practically overruled the provisions of the Decemviral law. The authors of the new jurisprudence during the whole process of its formation professed the most sedulous respect for the letter of the Code. They were merely explaining it, deciphering it, bringing out its full meaning; but then in the result, by piecing texts together, by adjusting the law to states of fact which actually presented themselves and by speculating on its possible application to others which might occur, by introducing principles of interpretation derived from the exegesis of other written documents which fell under their observation, they educed a variety of canons which had never been dreamed of by the compilers of the Twelve Tables and which were in truth rarely or never to be found there.[185]

In establishing their writings as secondary authorities, the Irish law commentators were able to change and expand legal principles. Through the attachment of the secondary to the primary text, the later medieval jurists continued to propagate a fiction that the law had not changed and that they were merely expounding and clarifying it.

One commentary that allows for changes more openly than most is Giolla na Naomh Mac Aodhagáin's late thirteenth-century precis of the Irish law of obligation. Mac Niocaill says that there are indications that it attained the status of a standard text.[186] Katharine Simms provides another useful example of the expansion of meaning to be found in a commentary in *Uraicecht Becc*.[187] The canonical text itself dates to about the ninth

---

[185] Sir Henry Sumner Maine, *Ancient Law: Its connection with the early history of society and its relation to modern ideas*, Oxford University Press, London, 1861 (1954 reprint) p. 28.

[186] Mac Niocaill, 'Aspects of Irish Law in the Late Thirteenth Century', pp. 30-31.

[187] Simms, *From Kings to Warlords*, p. 80.

century[188] and states that the honour price of a man's wife, his son who supports him, and his *rechtaire*[189] (if he is a king) or his deputy abbot (if he is an ecclesiastical head) is half the level of his own honour price. In a fourteenth-century manuscript, a Middle Irish commentary says that a king may have more than one *rechtaire* and these must share the half honour price. He also has servants of higher status which are to be protected by the full honour price of the king. In longer commentaries in the *Yellow Book of Lecan* and the *Book of Ballymote* all manner of hirelings are mentioned in addition. Simms shows how the later Irish rulers had a greater need for administrative staff; these commentaries are, then, good examples of the way in which the old law could be kept and expanded in line with contemporary needs.

Gearoid Mac Niocaill in a discussion of the entitlements of the finder of lost property, provides a further example of how the meaning of the old text may be changed.[190] He demonstrates that the commentaries on the classical text are expansive, with some of the stipulations finding no support in any of the classical texts. Without going into intricate details, it is useful to note that Mac Niocaill concludes that the two commentaries in question:

> ...fit in with the indications of other texts as to what was happening in the post-classical period of Irish law: a gradual extension of the power of the king and lord, and a corresponding reduction of the commoners to a uniformly dependent status largely derived from the base clientship of classical Irish law.[191]

As to the dates of these commentaries, Mac Niocaill notes the problems involved in dating, nevertheless he states that one (found in a mid-fourteenth-century manuscript) must date from the late twelfth century onwards and the other could be anywhere between the late tenth and the sixteenth century.[192] The point is, however, that the commentaries were a means through which the import of an ancient text could be broadened in accordance with changes in society.

---

[188] [See now Liam Breatnach, *A Companion to the Corpus Iuris Hibernici*, Dublin Institute for Advanced Studies, Dublin, 2005, p. 316.]

[189] A *rechtaire* is a seneschal.

[190] Gearoid Mac Niocaill, 'Jetsam, Treasure Trove and the Lord's Share in Medieval Ireland', *Irish Jurist*, 6 (1971) pp. 105-107.

[191] *Ibid.*, p. 107.

[192] *Ibid.*

A recent article by O'Corráin, Breatnach and Breen shows that the Irish jurists were willing to incorporate maxims of the Canon law as added authority for the legal provision they were interpreting, or situation they were trying to cover.[193] One important tract where this may be seen is found in Egerton 88 where the Canon law is quoted in Latin in a tract modifying old legal maxims relating to circumstances of church and state. O'Grady cites O'Curry as believing that there is nothing in the language of the tract to justify giving it a date of composition earlier than the twelfth century.[194] This is noteworthy because it shows the willingness of the later jurists to incorporate material from a source other than the ancient legal tracts. Further it sees this other source as authoritative. Simms says:

> This willingness to use thirteenth and fourteenth-century canon law to remodel what is sometimes thought of as the sacrosanct and immemorial corpus of traditional Irish custom (*féineachas*) was quite compatible with the Old Irish system of 'three judgments', and with the assertion at the beginning of *Uraicecht Becc*: 'The judgment of a lord, however, it is based on them all, on maxims and precedents and scriptural citations.' According to the writers of the Old Irish tracts, those pre-Christian customs of the Irish people which had been accepted by Patrick and handed on to later generations were based on natural law (*recht aicnid*), that is, on God's moral order as intuitively perceived by 'just men' before the faith. This view is maintained in the later commentaries, crediting native Irish custom with an underlying universality which meant it could be usefully discussed and analysed in terms of the *ius commune*, the internationally accepted standards of civil and canon law.[195]

The manuscripts also incorporate some principles derived from English common law. To mention Giolla na Naomh Mac Aodhagáin again, his text which renders an Old Irish corpus into modern Irish, shows some important borrowings from the common law.[196]

CONVENTIONS

The preservation of a written text relies also on the conventions which surround it. The continued adherence to the Australian Constitution might

---

[193] D. O'Corráin, L. Breatnach and A. Breen, 'The Laws of the Irish', *Peritia,* 3. (1984) p. 431.

[194] O'Grady, *Catalogue of Irish Manuscripts*, p. 95-96. The copy is in the hand of Domhnall O'Davoren and is dated 1569 and can be found in AL IV, p. 372.

[195] Simms, 'The brehons of later medieval Ireland', p. 71.

[196] Mac Niocaill, 'The interaction of laws', pp. 105-9.

seem antiquarian if we did not know of these. The conventions surrounding the Irish law manuscripts are unfortunately almost entirely lost to us. We can only see the way the texts remained relevant to the present through the interpretative techniques used on the text. James L. Kugel in the context of Biblical interpretation, points out that what the 'process of interpretation involves, what it claims to be doing, and what is considered to be an adequate realisation of its aims all tend to vary depending on the conventions surrounding the act itself.'[197] Nevertheless we should be aware of the theoretical way in which conventions may allow a seemingly irrelevant text to remain relevant.

James Boyd White argues that there is an 'invisible discourse' of the law – that is, the unstated conventions by which the language of the law operates, unstated conventions which underlie the law and are part of the legal culture.[198] Thus when we see legal rules which are apparently maintained, even though they cannot have operated in their society, we cannot assume that they were irrelevant; this is because we cannot wholly retrieve the legal culture which gave them meaning. The Irish legal culture, although based on written texts, was largely an oral one. The comment of Richard Stanihurst in 1577 perhaps gives some indication of the oral nature of Irish legal proceedings which is attested elsewhere:

> Other lawyers they haue lyable to certaine families, which after the custome of the countrey determine & judge causes. These consider of wrongs offered and receyued among their neighbours: if it be murther, felony, or trespasse, all is remedied by composition (except the grudge of parties seeke revenge) and the tyme they haue to spare from spoyling and preding, they lightly bestowe in parling about such matters. The breighon (so they call this kinde of lawyer) sitteth on a banke, the lordes and gentlemen at variance round about him, and then they proceede.[199]

We can expect that there were myriad unwritten conventions surrounding the use of the texts. If, alongside a written constitution, Australia can have a prime minister by convention alone, then we can presume that Irish legal culture also had conventions making their texts relevant in the present.

The change that we can observe in the manuscripts is only an indication of what must have occurred in practice. For as White argues, law is a culture of argument and interpretation which gives life and

---

197 Kugel, 'Early Interpretation', p. 28.

198 James Boyd White, *Heracles' Bow: Essays on the Rhetoric and Poetics of the Law*, University of Wisconsin Press, Wisconsin, 1985 p. 63.

199 L. Miller and E. Power, *Holinsheds Irish chronicle 1577*, Dublin, 1979 pp. 114-115. See also Nerys Patterson, 'Brehon Law in Late Medieval Ireland', p. 48.

meaning to rules.[200] For the proceedings of the late medieval Irish legal system, were probably largely, if not almost exclusively, oral in nature. We have some information about the use of the texts in litigation but this evidence is limited (as indeed is our evidence about litigation in general). Unfortunately, the available evidence only comes from the sixteenth and seventeenth centuries when Irish law was in its last stages of survival after the Tudor reconquest.

Gearoid Mac Niocaill notes that two tracts by Dubhaltach Mac Firbhisigh from 1671 describe the system of pleading that was observed.[201] The advocate would begin by stating the case in question or by refuting the accuracy of the other party's case. This would be followed with a string of quotes, usually from the ancient law texts and sometimes with glosses and commentaries to further embellish them. This system is borne out, according to Mac Niocaill, by three pleadings which survive from the sixteenth century. He says that characteristic of these quotes is that they are irrelevant to the issue to be decided, although he concedes that the commentary sometimes is relevant.[202] From this he concludes it was likely that a pleader stumbled on a relevant quotation by accident rather than design.[203] However, Máirín Ní Dhonnchadha says:

> The citation of brocards from the canonical texts by pleaders in the later period has occasionally been dismissed by modern scholars as window-dressing and it has been argued that the pleaders could have had only a vague idea of the content of these citations. But as Mac Niocaill has pointed out in his discussion of the sixteenth-century pleadings, even where the citations are not wholly apposite to the case in hand, the commentary frequently shows that they are being treated as relevant: the interpretation of the authority quoted, whether true to the original or not, is *imposed* by the advocate. It follows that any divergence between the application and the canonical text cannot be treated as proof of the pleader's ignorance of the language of the original.[204]

---

[200] Boyd-White, *Heracles' Bow*, p. 98.

[201] Gearóid Mac Niocaill, 'Notes on Litigation in Late Irish Law', *Irish Jurist*, 2 (1967) pp. 304-305.

[202] This conclusion was earlier proposed by Binchy who says that native decisions from the 16th century show evidence of citations from the old tracts but these have little relevance to the actual decision being made. Binchy, 'Ancient Irish Law', pp. 89-90.

[203] Mac Niocaill, 'Notes on Litigation in Late Irish Law', p. 304.

[204] Máirín Ní Dhonnchadha, 'An Address to a Student of Law', in O Corráin, Breatnach and McCone (eds.), *Sages, Saints and Storytellers: Celtic Studies in Honour of Professor James Carney,* An Sagart, Maynooth, 1989 pp. 161-162.

This gives some indication of how the conventions surrounding the use of the texts in litigation could allow the old texts to be applied in the present.

Of course no legal culture is unchanging. As social and cultural change occurs over time, legal culture experiences change also. Thus the context in which a legal text has meaning changes. White argues that as a text was written to have meaning in a specific cultural context, when this context changes a difficulty arises as to how this meaning is now to be found.[205] However, the text, he says, does not lose its meaning, but its meaning necessarily changes. This is because as our language and culture changes, we acquire material for asking new questions. The text may then reveal new answers, and thereby give a new meaning to the text.[206] How each generation chose to treat the texts, and to what new questions the texts could provide the answers, we can not know. Their importance is attested by their continued attention till the final demise of the Irish law schools and legal system after the Tudor reconquest. For, as Mazzeo asserts, it is only texts of a sacred and normative character which demand and receive the attention of the intellectual and spiritual élite.[207]

CONCLUSION

Glossing and commenting operates on two levels. On one level it seeks to direct our attention to the canonical text; arguing that in it lies a fixed authoritative meaning which can be retrieved and applied in a changed society. This secondary material is thus instrumental in establishing the authority of the texts on which all legal decisions must be based. It argues that interpretation is merely mechanical, that it discovers and gives affect to the 'original' meaning of the text. By establishing the text as authority, the secondary material seeks to remove the interpretation of the text from the prevailing social and political context in which it exists.

On another level the glosses and commentaries were very important methods of textual interpretation, allowing the text to accommodate social and cultural change whilst maintaining the fictions that the text was immutable. These methods were not peculiar to Ireland. The old law could be 'translated' or 'interpreted' into more modern language and a changed society. Or by providing a secondary hierarchy of authorities to be consulted as to the 'correct' interpretation of the canonical text, the late

---

[205] Boyd-White, *Heracles' Bow*, p. 88.

[206] *Ibid.*, p. 89.

[207] Mazzeo, *Varieties of Interpretation*, p. 115.

medieval Irish jurists could allow the law to develop. Thus, what appears to many to be an antiquarian technique may in fact be seen as a method to establish the authority of texts (and thereby legal decisions) in the present, and a way of adapting an authoritative old text to a changed society.

Of course much interpretation must have occurred in the context of day-to-day litigation. Authoritative decisions could rest on interpretations of a text whose authority was established. But because texts exist in a wider legal culture, we cannot expect to find all the means by which the texts were interpreted for the present. Texts derive their meaning largely from the culture in which they exist. Thus, the conventions which surround the law texts, and their use, are another way in which the past may be reinterpreted to give the texts life in the present.

IV. LEGAL EDUCATION

He cannot bind who is not able to pass judgment...

Gloss on *Senchas Már*, AL Vol. 1, p.297.

This Fenechus or Brehon Lawe, is none other but the civill lawe, which the Brehons had in an obscure and unknown language, which none could understand except those that studied in the open schools they had....

Note added in Mageoghegan's version of the Annals of Clonmacnoise for the year of 1318. Cited in John O'Donovan (ed. & trans.) Annals of the Kingdom of Ireland by the Four Masters, Hodges, Smith, & Co., Dublin, 1854. (A.M.S. Press, Inc. N.Y. 1966.)

A 'fixed' text, whether a written or oral text, interpreted for the present, implies the existence of interpreters. If we allow for significant scope for change through interpretation, then we see that much power resides in the hands of the interpreters. Goodrich emphasises the important role of the interpreter:

> The written code of law functions to conceal the source of law as much as it purports to reveal the substantive laws themselves. The code establishes the social power of a priestly group of interpreters of the law and if we trace very briefly the history of legal codifications as sources of law, we find that the power of the code is time and again located in the hidden and ambiguous character of its source and the correlatively priestly status of its interpreters. The two categories, those of source and interpretation, are intimately and enduringly linked, it being the hidden and sacred character of the source of law that determines the rigidity and authoritarianism of its interpretation.[208]

THE LAW MANUSCRIPTS AND LEGAL EDUCATION

The surviving Irish law manuscripts are almost exclusively the products of the secular schools of law which emerged in the fourteenth century. It is in these schools that what were considered the necessary skills of a trained lawyer were taught. There is consequently a very close connection

---

[208] Goodrich, *Reading the Law*, pp.27-28.

between the manuscript production and legal instruction. The law manuscripts not only demonstrate interpretive technique but, I believe, may be examined as 'manuals' of interpretive technique: that is, in the context of their role in training interpreters.

As we have seen, the transition to a secular site for manuscript production and legal education shows a deliberate choice to continue and even revive the style and content of manuscripts produced in the twelfth century. The choice exhibited a deliberate commitment to the 'old', to the 'texts' of the past. At the same time there was an expansion in the geographical and political area over which Irish law had jurisdiction. To establish and maintain this jurisdiction one supposes an effectively trained legal profession to have been essential. As the law texts appear to have been at the basis of this legal education it follows that comprehensive knowledge of them was probably very important for a well trained lawyer. For if the canonical texts were to remain fixed, it must have been important that well trained lawyers existed to interpret them, both in the law schools and in legal practice.

The Irish law schools in which the law manuscripts were produced had a great commitment to the canonical seventh- and eighth-century texts. This commitment is exemplified by the author of a poem composed at the beginning of the period of transition from a monastic to secular environment for manuscript production. The author almost anticipates charges of antiquarianism, and stresses that learning the old texts is crucial to the study and practice of the lawyer in the present:

> 7. Learn every old precedent here, though it be an old precedent it is not objectionable; it is on its premise you will best give judgment if you consider every aspect, I believe.

> 18. Effort (alone) does not make for judgment, in Irish law the matter is not trifling; learn and apply to everyone the forceful, ready old testimony.[209]

The poem is unique in being an address to 'the student of law' in modern language. It is thought fairly certain that it was written by Giolla na Naomh Mac Aodhagáin who died in 1309. It was almost certainly written in the late thirteenth or the beginning of the fourteenth century a period in which there is little documentary evidence for legal teaching. Most of the available material on late medieval Irish law comes from the centuries after the transition of manuscript production in the thirteenth century from

---

[209] Ní Dhonnchadha, 'An Address to a Student of Law', p. 169.

a monastic to a secular environment.[210] Written in the transition period the poem provides advice which seems to have been followed throughout the following three hundred years of Irish legal activity. For, until the demise of the last law school in the seventeenth century, the Irish law manuscripts continued to be produced and studied in the law schools.

LEGAL EDUCATION: SUBSTANCE VERSUS METHOD

With such a commitment to the old texts and the need for an effective legal education, the question presents itself as to how the law texts were to be used in providing, at least part of, this education.

It is a commonplace of legal education that it is the central function of a law school to teach the method of the law; the substance of the law is but a secondary consideration. That is not to deny that the substance of the law is important, yet it cannot be described in a full and complete manner. If the law could be described as a list of definable rules there would be little need for a law school. These rules could be learnt and entry to the profession regulated by an examination of one's knowledge of these rules. That such is not the case is clearly evident. One cannot easily divine what the law is in a given situation for, despite the claims of the legal formalists, the law is not certain. The role of the law school is to teach the method of interpretation: the way in which the law is to be understood, developed and applied within that legal system. Legal education introduces the student to a specialised legal language, a knowledge of the texts and the hierarchy in which they exist as well as training in important interpretative methods. It teaches the appropriate discourse within which practitioners must operate: what is acceptable and what is not.

LEARNING THE LANGUAGE OF THE LAW

The language of the law texts was difficult because of its antiquity. Nevertheless the attachment to the old texts meant that the language of the old texts had to be learnt. Learning the language was essential if it was to be manipulated and the principles of the old text applied. In itself, this concentration on old legal language is not an anomaly nor necessarily evidence of antiquarianism: for instance, the use of archaisms, of law

---

[210] *Ibid.*, p. 159.

French, and Latin loan words is still very prevalent in the modern common law systems. As Goodrich asserts,

> [t]o learn the law is to learn an archaic and specialised vocabulary and syntax.[211]

Giolla na Naomh Mac Aodhagáin stresses the importance of learning the archaic and specialised language:

> 4. The literary language whose thrust is not self-evident or superficial and the noble reading aloud – for ardent judges and bards, they are the keys which release locks.

The student of law as a potential practitioner of the law, must become conversant in the language which the legal system requires. This is a general requirement of legal education and not peculiar to the Irish. The language of the law is a means of controlling legal interpretation – it is only interpretations which are framed in this language which are acceptable to the legal system. The system thus restricts interpretation and application of legal texts to those trained in the language system of the law.

The language of the law, says Goodrich, is inseparable from the formalist notion of interpretation. Legal language seeks to establish the law as a 'closed' language system: a system whereby legal meanings derive entirely from the legal 'world', and not from the societal context within which the law exists. Legal meanings are thereby seen as independent, and thus objective and authoritative. Their inability to be coloured by context means that interpretation and application is merely mechanical. And as such, interpreters merely apply authoritative legal meanings through authorised legal language – authority in the legal system thus derives not from the interpreters of the texts, but from its authoritatively interpreted texts.

LAW TEXTS AND LEGAL LEARNING: LAW AS A LITERARY PURSUIT

Law, argues Goodrich, is a specialised literary pursuit, not empirical in nature, in which the student acquires knowledge of legal texts. The student must first learn the techniques that are relevant to finding and interpreting the law. The ability to engage in such interpretation requires knowledge of the materials of the legal system which include not just the institutional

---

[211] Goodrich, 'Law and Language', p. 188.

framework but, in a system based at least in part on writing, on the texts of the legal system.[212] Legal education requires gaining a knowledge of those texts: how to find the law, how authoritative that 'law' is, and to how apply it.

A knowledge of the authoritative status of texts, and how they are to fit into the hierarchy of texts authoritatively interpreted, is critical.[213] What distinguishes the discipline of law from other textual disciplines, is this way of reading the law. This 'reading' leads to the 'control of behaviour by reference to binding texts authoritatively interpreted'.[214] The more authoritative a text, the more important it is that it be observed.[215] Thus it is a very important aspect of legal education that the authoritative status of a text be imparted and learned, and this involves a knowledge of the hierarchy in which these authoritative texts existed. There are many different hierarchies to be observed. In the previous chapter we saw that secondary writing seeks to ascribe ultimate authority to the canonical text, presenting itself as a secondary authority. Even if in practice the secondary writing is more authoritative, it is important for the underlying fictions of the legal system that there be a commitment to the authority of the primary writing. There is also a hierarchy between different texts and between different parts of texts.

It is clear that the *Senchas Már* was regarded as the principal legal text in this period. It had already been placed in order by the Old Irish period. This is shown by the fact that different manuscripts, with entirely different glossing, follow the same order.[216] In the later law schools the *Senchas Már* was divided into three parts and this division may go back to the Old Irish period.[217] The order has been reconstructed but there is some doubt about it particularly regarding the last part; it would also seem that there are additional texts from this part which have not survived.[218] Binchy says:

---

[212] Goodrich, *Reading the Law*, p. 91.

[213] *Ibid.*, p. 91.

[214] *Ibid.*, p. 91.

[215] *Ibid.*, p. 92.

[216] Kelly, *A Guide to Early Irish Law*, p. 243.

[217] *Ibid.*, p. 243.

[218] *Ibid.*, pp. 243-245.

> Its (the *Senchas Már's*) reception into all the schools (or at least those in which our extant manuscripts were written) meant that it took pride of place in the legal curriculum....[219]

Commentators referred to the overriding authority of the *Senchas Már:*

> The law of the Senchus is a law which excels and overtops every law; as the top of a tree overtops its trunk, so the law of the Senchus overtops every law.[220]

The *Senchas Már* was copied more often, and more copiously glossed and commented on than other texts. It was not however a singular legal authority. Binchy says:

> Yet the other collections were not entirely superseded. Later jurists drew freely on them for purposes of quotation and comparison, and more or less complete (though generally unglossed) copies of some of the principal tracts have survived.[221]

What was important was that a student know how the different texts stood in relation to one another. And not only this, but the student should also know what is of value in a particular tract and what is not. As Giolla na Naomh Mac Aodhagáin advised:

> 17. Teach and admonish your family to look evenly at the tracts; adhere to what is of value and worth in them, take note of their impropriety and do not declare it. [222]

An example of the distinction between the good and the bad parts of a text, is perhaps found in the fifteenth- and sixteenth-century manuscript of Egerton 90, in which a remark appended to a section of commentary points out that:

> This is out of the 'yellow authority' and this 'locus' is bad.[223]

---

[219] Binchy, *Bretha Nemed*, p. 5.

[220] *A.L.*, Vol. I, p. 33.

[221] Binchy, *Bretha Nemed*, p. 5.

[222] Ní Dhonnchadha, 'An Address to a Student of Law', p. 169.

[223] O'Grady, *Catalogue of Irish Manuscripts*, p. 78. This reference is found on f. 9 of the third fragment of Egerton 90.

A knowledge of the texts and their relative authority is thus one very important facet of legal training. Another crucial part of legal education is that the methodology of the law be learnt.

ACADEMIC EXERCISES

In accepting that the glosses and commentaries can have had no direct relevance to the practical application of the law, Kelly asserts that they must:

> ...be regarded as ingenious academic exercises, solely for internal consumption in the schools, where they presumably helped to develop the forensic skills of aspiring lawyers.[224]

But whether the manuscripts were for internal consumption only is debatable. It is significant that Kelly sees for them a role in developing the forensic skills of aspiring lawyers. The connection that the development of these skills has with the practice of the law should not be underestimated. As Ní Dhonnchadha says of the address to a student of law:

> In the text, the role envisaged for the student is professional rather than academic. His education in the canonical law-tracts is to be put to use in a practical way in the deciding of legal cases. Whether he will act in the capacity of judge or advocate is not spelt out but as the ability to fulfil the higher role must have depended on both educational qualification and professional repute, the ambitious student will obviously aim for this.[225]

Despite the paucity of documentary evidence, there are some scattered indications that the Irish manuscripts were used as a source of authority in litigation. Mac Niocaill in his discussion on litigation in late medieval Irish law provides evidence from surviving pleading documents, and two tracts by Dubhaltach Mac Firbhisigh written in 1671, about the technique of pleading a case. It appears that it involved the use of a 'barrage of quotations mainly from classical i.e. early Irish – law texts, with or without an accompaniment of quoted glosses or commentary to cover their nakedness'.[226] Without entering into that debate I believe that there are

---

[224] Kelly, *A Guide to Early Irish Law*, p. 252.

[225] Ní Dhonnchadha, 'An Address to the Student of Law', p. 161.

[226] Mac Niocaill, 'Notes on Litigation in Late Irish Law', p. 304. It is interesting that in Wales also, arbitrators who called themselves judges (barnwyr) were chosen for their knowledge of Welsh law; and supported their judgments by references to the

good reasons for regarding many of the more technical commentaries as primarily academic exercises to teach legal method. And of course this is crucial to the practice of law.

INTERPRETATIVE TECHNIQUES

Legal education requires a gaining of knowledge as to how to apply legal texts to complex 'fact situations'. And such a process is at heart an exercise in how to use language in a way countenanced by the legal system: one uses acceptable words defined through the use of prescribed authorities. The ability to distinguish is vital to the application of the law. A gloss on the *Senchas Már* perhaps gives some indication of this:

> He cannot bind who is not able to pass judgment i.e. he cannot truly bind it on stay with notice in the hand of the debtor, unless he is a person who is able to give an opinion as to its lawfulness. He cannot pass judgment unless he can distinguish i.e. he cannot give an opinion as to its lawfulness.[227]

Similarly:

> NO PERSON IS QUALIFIED TO PLEAD A CAUSE AT THE HIGH COURT UNLESS HE IS SKILLED IN EVERY DEPARTMENT OF LEGAL SCIENCE.
>
> That is, he is not qualified to manage the cause in taking distress for the cause, or covenant, unless he has good skill in knowledge of every stay and notice i.e. the four stays and the four delays in pound and the two notices, i.e. a notice of one day upon him whose house is the road, who, from what is known of the meaning of the first part of the law written by the poets, is to be pursued to the border of the territory, and seized by the collar at the frontier of the territory, unless a native surety come to his relief, and if such come, he shall pay for him i.e. he is seized by the breast...S.D.[228]

Distinctions are constantly being made in the commentaries. For example:

> What is the difference between these and where it is said in the other place....
>
> The wool is undervalued in the other text, and overvalued here....

---

law texts. R.R. Davies, 'The Administration of Law in Medieval Wales: The Role of the Ynad Cwmwd (Judex Patrie)', p. 261.

[227] *A.L.*, Vol. I, p. 297.

[228] *A.L.*, Vol. II, p. 89. Text and commentary.

> And it is from a native to a stranger in the other text or from the stranger to the native; and it is from a native to a stranger here...[229]

The charge of excessive casuistry has been levelled at the commentaries on the law texts. And yet this may be understood as just such an exercise in the ability to distinguish. Many of the commentaries consist of lists of every different possible and impossible situation which might arise, and the legal solution which would be applied. If we do not assume that these should accord with legal reality, but approach them as a way of teaching the legal method of distinguishing (of using the language of the law), then the late medieval Irish law manuscripts are not necessarily the activity of antiquarians. Casuistry may in fact be seen as a very useful tool in legal education. It is a method used in modern law schools, whereby often seemingly unreal and impossible fact situations are given for the student to divine the legal principles applicable and to see the legal results of different approaches and small differences of fact. The more ludicrous the facts, the clearer will be the legal principle which the system requires to be taught. The student may learn and apply methods of interpretation, learning to manipulate facts and language to achieve a desired result. This is done in a way which has no effect on anyone in the real world – it is a controlled learning environment.

The casuistry of the commentaries may also be understood if we see the manuscripts as being the repositories of legal principles. Robin Chapman Stacey advances the view that the legal tracts were to be regarded as a source of principles to be consulted, not for specific rules applicable to a given case, but as a guide to the principles to be at the basis of a legal decision. She argues that by having deliberately elastic concepts these could be reinterpreted in the light of present standards and expectations. Thus there was not a need to replace the old law with new provisions because 'there was life in the old law yet.'[230] Learning to apply principles to different fact situations teaches the student to manipulate the texts: to learn how to apply a principle and find an acceptable legal answer

---

[229] *A.L.*, Vol. V, p. 81.

[230] Robin Chapman Stacey, *Lawbooks and Legal Enforcement in Medieval Ireland and Wales,* PhD dissertation, Yale University, May 1986 p. 287. It is interesting that Stacey arrives at this conclusion whilst still accepting the received view that the later jurists had an 'unquestioning commitment ... to the preservation of linguistic and historical archaisms', that the texts were 'set in stone' so that the later jurists composed 'fantastically inaccurate' glosses on tracts irrelevant to their own society and written in a language they could not understand.

which ostensibly accords with the letter of the authoritative text. Goodrich believes this may be a feature of any written law. He says:

> The written law may be deliberately vague, it may be archaic, it may not deal with relevant local issues. Its role, in short, may be one of enunciating principles and of stipulating the general scheme of desirable social relationships either without governing or without directly stipulating the conditions for the resolution of particular disputes. In such circumstances the code of written law is either substantively irrelevant (a relic) or one of several factors loosely limiting the choice of decision in the particular case. In the latter instance the legal tradition has most generally resorted to the courts, the judiciary and customary law to fill the gaps or to interpret the written law.[231]

Once again we see the importance of the well trained interpreter.

Legal principles may be applied by analogy. The fanciful casuistry found in the commentaries might have been used by way of comparison with a situation to be resolved in real life. A comment at the beginning of a section describing the circumstances of the compilation of the *Senchas Már* perhaps alludes to this:

> Understand ye now that the author could not mention everything [i.e. every particular case]: but of whatsoever particular 'species' [i.e. case] he shall have treated, he has directed that every analogous case be decided accordingly, even as the following laws declare.[232]

The use of analogy in making judgments is also mentioned in a gloss:

> From true judgments according to analogy i.e. according to the true analogous judgments i.e. all cases similar, but which had not been brought forward.[233]

By showing that there are points of analogy between an example in the text and the situation to be decided in real life, a legal principle may be applied. Through analogy the 'fixed' law texts may be mechanically applied in the present. Thus the ability to make a skilful use of analogy is also an important part of legal education.

A similar use of analogy provides interesting parallels between education in the common law in England of the late Middle Ages and Irish legal

---

[231] Goodrich, *Reading the Law*, p. 61.

[232] O'Grady, *Catalogue of Irish Manuscripts*, p. 98. This is from f.39b Col 2 of Egerton 88.

[233] *A.L.*, Vol. I, p. 209.

learning of the same period. J.H. Baker in his discussion of the Inns of Court in the fifteenth and sixteenth centuries says that in teaching the law,

> The readers' usual technique was to list example upon example in illustration of the subject matter. The more examples, and the more comprehensive the set of examples, the better. It does not seem to have mattered too much whether they were examples ever likely to be met with in the real world, though of course the law-teacher's most unlikely academic fantasies have a habit of coming true. The prime purpose seems to have been to exercise the mind, in showing how the principles worked in hypothetical situations, rather than to explore new doctrine, criticise old doctrine, or open up loopholes.[234]

Baker further says that:

> [e]ven if some of these cases never occurred in practice, the readers' attempts to analyse and rationalise doctrine must have borne abundant fruit.[235]

Thurneysen's conclusion that the late medieval Irish law commentaries in particular contain

> ...elaborate calculations, minute casuistry, and strange constructions which often lead to quite impossible results and can never have had any significance for the practical administration of the law...[236]

is thus indeed questionable.

THE STUDY OF POETRY, HISTORY AND CANON LAW

The study of Irish law did not occur in a compartmentalised legal world. Irish legal study took place in contact with other fields of study. This contact was also very important in producing a well trained lawyer and not necessarily a further indication of antiquarian tendencies. The study of law and poetry often went together. The Mac Fhlannchadha and Mac Aodhagáin law schools taught both law and poetry while the other family law schools are described in the annals as teaching law only.[237] Giolla na Naomh Mac Aodhagáin in his poem gives the advice that law students

---

[234] J.H. Baker, "The Inns of Court and Legal Doctrine', in *Lawyers and Laymen*, p. 276.

[235] *Ibid.*, p.280.

[236] Quoted in Binchy, 'Irish History and Irish Law: II', p. 32.

[237] Simms, 'The brehons of later medieval Ireland', p. 63.

study not just the law-tracts themselves. They should make additional study of the Old Irish kingship tracts, the teachings of Cormac mac Airt and the *Audacht Morainn,* as well as of history and poetry.[238]

Katharine Simms argues that there are practical and theoretical reasons for the later medieval jurists to study both poetry and law. Of the practical benefits, she says a teaching *ollamh* or commentarist would have gained much through the linguistic training of the bardic poet. This would have enabled greater familiarity with the Old Irish original. A good understanding of this was very important for an expert. She says that many of the mythical judgments presuppose a knowledge of old tales and sagas and historians were often called as expert witnesses in disputes over land.[239] On a more theoretical level, the study of poetry and law was also attractive, for, in the Irish legal system, the broader one's learning, the higher was one's honour price. This is evidenced in both Old Irish text and the later commentary of *Uraicecht Becc.* The text states:

> Who has one art, let him have one *dire*; he who has many arts, let him have many *dires*: it increases nobility.

The commentary refers to 'an advocate whom judgment encounters' who was also a poet of the third grade, who consequently had an honour price of twelve rather than nine cows.[240]

This same commentary requires that a court advocate have a good knowledge of customary law and poetry as opposed to a junior advocate who need only be familiar with the law tracts. The former was likened to the Old Irish judge both in matters concerning the laity and the poets. The senior 'advocate whom judgment encounters' is likened by the commentarist to the Old Irish judge of three speeches: law, poetry and Latin learning.[241] Simms believes that, in the Mac Fhlannchadha and Mac Aodhagáin law schools, although some commentarists had knowledge of Latin learning to the extent that it related to Irish law, training was really only available in the two speeches of poetry and customary law.[242]

It is said that the Irish jurists understood their tracts as being historical in nature.[243] The importance of an historical background to the

---

[238] *Ibid.,* p. 63. Ní Dhonnchadha, 'An Address to a Student of Law', p. 162.

[239] Simms, 'The brehons of later medieval Ireland', p. 65.

[240] *Ibid.,* p. 65.

[241] *Ibid.*

[242] *Ibid.,* p. 74.

[243] Stacey, *Lawbooks and Legal Enforcement in Medieval Ireland and Wales*, p. 19.

legal system in which a lawyer operates is often stressed. In common law learning today, for example, it is not possible to understand the concepts which underlie land law without an understanding as to how they have developed from feudal times. Mackintosh asserts:

> ...It is now admitted on all hands that a full understanding of the law is, even for practical purposes, inseparable from a knowledge of its history.[244]

Knowledge of history was similar to that of poetry. Of the place of history in Irish legal learning, E.J. Gwynn says:

> Whatever the contents of this tract [Bretha Nemed] may have been, it must have held a high place in the curriculum of students of law, if we may trust a remark in the preface to Mac Firbis's Genealogies which is quoted by O'Curry, MS Material 575, and translated, *ibid*. 219: *ni breitheamh nach Seanchaidh, agas ni Seanchaid nach bretheamh i mBreathaibh Nimeadh .i. leabhar deridh saothair na Seanchadh, agas na mbretheamhan bheos*, 'a man could not be a judge without being an historian; and he is not an historian without being a judge in the *Brethibh Nimhedh*, that is the last Books of the works (study) of the *Seanchaidhe* or historians, and of the Judges themselves'.[245]

The historical perspective on the law which the old texts could give was, similar to the study of poetry, important for legal education in the present.

Some of the Irish jurists also received education in Latin and the Canon law. Katharine Simms shows how in later medieval times there existed local schools which taught university subjects. The owner often took the title of 'master'. In 1384 there is mentioned Master John MacGiolla Choisgle, 'erenagh and parson of Airech-Brosga [in Fermanagh], an approved lecturer in both laws and especially of the canon law'.[246] Simms suggests that the student of Brehon law could also have attended one of the Latin schools particularly because many of them entered the church.[247] There was also acquaintance with Latin fostered in the law schools as is indicated by the Latin found in the manuscripts. This was important because Canon law was seen as another valid source for law.[248] The importance of these other studies was to produce lawyers with

---

[244] J. Mackintosh, *Roman Law in Modern Practice*, p. 27.

[245] E.J. Gwynn, 'An Old-Irish tract on the Priviledges and Responsibilities of Poets', *Eriu*, Vol XIII (1942), p. 7n.

[246] Simms, 'The brehons of later medieval Ireland', p. 69.

[247] *Ibid*., p. 70.

[248] See discussion in previous chapter.

a broad education, a knowledge of their culture and good linguistic skills essential to legal practice.

A curious fact which remains is that the only copies of some tracts are to be found in manuscripts which are not legal manuscripts. As such they appear to be part of a collection of old manuscripts compiled for antiquarian reasons. This is apparently explained by a commentary in *Uraicecht Becc.* Katharine Simms says:

> ...those engaged in the four practical professions, the braziers, carpenters, physicians and smiths, had a financial interest in studying the customary laws applying to their own skills...A craftsman who was thus learned was qualified to pass judgment himself regarding the payments he was entitled to as the reward of his labour, as long as the proceedings were witnessed by a trained lawyer. Unlearned craftsman needed a brehon to pass judgment for them, and the judge then obtained a twelfth of the whole as his traditional fee.[249]

This is why, Simms maintains, we find two Old Irish tracts relating to physicians in a fifteenth-century medical manuscript, and no more than excerpts from them in purely legal manuscripts. Thus even these texts were relevant to the present and not merely preserved for antiquarian reasons.

AN EFFECTIVE LEGAL EDUCATION?

The effectiveness of Irish legal education may perhaps be exemplified by the ease with which the jurists are credited in adapting to the English common law. In the sixteenth century Edmund Spenser complained that while Englishmen, himself included, found Irish law difficult to understand, the Irish were able to master the subtleties of the common law with relatively little difficulty. He said:

> ...they are for the most part so cautelous and wily headed, especially being men of so small experience and practice in law matters, that you would wonder whence they borrow such subtleties and sly shifts.[250]

---

[249] Simms, 'The brehons of later medieval Ireland', p. 62.

[250] Cited in Katharine Simms, 'The Legal Position of Irish Women in the Later Middle Ages', *Irish Jurist*, 10 (1975) p. 107.

CONCLUSION

Irish legal education after the transition from a monastic to secular environment was committed to the use of old texts. This use of the texts may be seen as important in educating the potential lawyer in a much changed and expanding legal system and further that this education in the old texts and the methods of interpreting them was important for the practice of law. Thus it was a present centred activity, because the legal system required a well trained legal profession and a profession which could skilfully develop and apply the canonical legal texts, and so keep them alive in the present.

It is also important that the fictions upon which textual interpretation and indeed the legal system depend are inculcated in the student. As Goodrich says:

> In one aspect, the entire process of socialisation into the legal institution, from entry into law school to membership of the profession itself, is an elaborate process of education into the manner and techniques of deference and respect for the authority of legal sources and the procedures and languages of its hierarchical organisational forms.[251]

---

[251] Goodrich, 'Law and Language', pp. 187-188.

V. PAST AND PRESENT

The search for origins is a common and intelligible, but doomed, project, since our notions of where we come from depend on our sense of where we are, and the past is invariably constructed in the image of the present.

Marion Campbell, 'Unending desire: Sidney's reinvention of petrarchan form in Astrophil and Stella', *Sir Philip Sidney and the Interpretation of Renaissance Culture: the Poet in his time and ours*, Waller and Moore (eds.), Croom Helm, London, 1984 p.84.

The Irish jurists had a great commitment to the texts of the past. The canonical texts were the basis of legal education and practice and the interpretative methods used arguably allowed these texts to remain relevant to their society. But the question presents itself: why such an attachment to the past? Why insist that the texts are immutable and stress that they are the wisdom of the ancients? Why, in the very time of political revival and transition from a monastic to secular legal context, was Giolla na Naomh Mac Aodhagáin so insistent that the Irish student look to the old texts, to the wisdom of the ancients as the basis of law?

Of the codification of Justinian it has been said:

> The greatest codification in the history of western law was a symbol of power and an object of reverence. It wrote down an archaic and alien law for political and ideological reasons, and that it subsequently became the object of an almost mystical awe had more to do with the political needs of the later western governments than it had to do with the substantive legal content of the codification as a whole.[252]

Similarly, I am interested in looking at the ideological and political role of the use of old texts.

USING THE PAST

The Irish law manuscripts use the past. The past takes the shape of ancient canonical law tracts which provide the basis for legal writing and copying in the late medieval period. The choice to use these texts, and the writing

---

[252] Goodrich, *Reading the Law*, p. 32.

style and method of interpretation used in the twelfth century, appears to be deliberate. It is generally accepted that these manuscripts exhibit a fixation with the past for the past's sake, that they are the work of antiquarians. The use of the past, so this view postulates, is an attempt to preserve the past.

But the past is potent. The use of the past reveals the concerns of the present and is an active creative force for the future. The past is not static. The preservation of fixed texts necessarily entails a negotiation with the past with a view to the present. The attempt to bridge the social and cultural gap between the past and the present (which as we have seen is what the preservation of these texts requires) is significant. We have already said that the texts which a society will choose to preserve will be those of intrinsic importance to their knowledge systems and value structures. What then was the intrinsic importance of the law tracts such that a definite decision to continue or revive their production was made? To whom were they important and why?

The process of the recreation of meaning of 'fixed' texts is inextricably involved with the use of the past to illuminate the problems of the present. In a society undergoing rapid change, the necessity to demonstrate continuity with the past becomes more immediate.[253] It is an activity which occurs constantly, but is occluded for ideological reasons. Demonstrating continuity with the past involves making culturally important texts able to be understood in the changed environment, while asserting a continuity with the society in which the texts originated.[254] Interpretative activity mediates the distance between the present and the records of the past.[255] Kim McCone says:

> Lévi-Strauss has suggested that so-called 'primitive' thought, as opposed to the modern western mode inherited from classical Greece via Rome, typically integrates past and present by means of a relatively static mytho-historical model that is primarily concerned with authorising various values and institutions regarded as essentially immutable thereafter. When actual and irresistible changes threaten to dislocate such a system, reintegration can only be achieved by modifying, recreating or (as in the rather special case of allegory) reinterpreting the past in the light of a new present. As

---

[253] Mazzeo, *Varieties of Interpretation*, p. 95.

[254] *Ibid.*, p. 95.

[255] *Ibid.*, p. 96.

Vansina puts it,"traditions are altered, more or less consciously, to fit in with the cultural values of the time".[256]

For a culture to be inherited it must be preserved; and to be preserved a constant and shifting reinterpretation of the past is required:

> for only interpretation can mediate between the past and present laden with the future.[257]

LAW, LEGITIMACY AND THE PAST

The use of the authority of the past in a legal context is recurrent. Mac Niocaill quotes S.E. Thorne in his book on Sir Edward Coke as saying:

> If we turn to the common law reports, particularly to the pages of Coke's Reports, nothing will be found there that labels itself "new". The cases cited most frequently are those decided by judges long in their graves...and every doctrine there set forth bears, prominently displayed, the stamp of approval of the ancient sages of the law...Occasionally the sages' stamp is authentic and the article genuine...But very often the stamp is bogus...

What is of interest then is not whether texts genuinely represent the past, but that they claim authority or legitimacy through use of the past. Bakhtin says:

> The authoritative word demands that we acknowledge it, that we make it our own: it binds us quite independent of any power it might have to persuade us internally; we encounter it with its authority already attached to it. The authoritative word is located in a distanced zone, organically connected with a past that is felt to be hierarchically higher. It is, so to speak, the word of the fathers. Its authority was already *acknowledged* in the past...It is given (it sounds) in lofty spheres, not those of familiar contact....[258]

The Irish legal system was thus not unusual in its use of the past. In the late medieval Irish law manuscripts there are several explicit statements to be found, particularly in the glosses, which seek to ascribe the authority of

[256] Kim McCone, *Pagan Past and Christian Present in Early Irish Literature*, An Sagart, 1990 (1991 reprint) p. 104.

[257] Mazzeo, *Varieties of Interpretation*, p. 110.

[258] M.M. Bakhtin, *The Dialogic Imagination*, (Edited by Michael Holquist, translated by Caryl Emerson and Michael Holquist) University of Texas Press, Austin, 1981 p. 342.

a passage by reference to the older book from which it derives. For example:

> This is the old reading of the same 'Yellow Book'...[259]
>
> That which follows down here is from the Senchus Book of O'Scoba...[260]
>
> ....in this case there is fastened upon them that stock which the books mention...[261]
>
> The implied duty of the grandfather, i.e. one sixth, or as far as great want; or the implied duty of every woman as it is said in the book called 'Cin'.[262]
>
> And every woman in general may give the presents which are mentioned in the book called 'Cin'...[263]

Several passages are also ascribed to a text referred to as S.D.[264]

The later Irish jurists insisted on maintaining the fiction that what they were doing was part of a continuous tradition, traceable to the wisdom of the ancients and thus to the ultimate authority of the legal texts and the legal system. In the poem of advice to law students, written by Giolla na Naomh Mac Aodhagáin in the period of transition and revival, much is made of the ancient sages who supposedly authored the poetico-legal 'wisdom texts', and the authority they could lend to the learning possessed by professional lawyers. For example:

> 8. Keep in mind noble Fiothal's charge to Flaithre who pacified hosts, since it is found in particular books, memorise it and guard it still.[265]
>
> 10. Relate the Instructions of Cormac ua Cuinn to Caibre of renowned name, and do not relate them fatuously – you will be called a sage.[266]

Of course, this was not an entirely continuous tradition linking back to these ancient sages, and the law texts were now being produced and used

---

[259] AL., Vol. II, p. 133. Commentary.

[260] AL., Vol. II, p. 135. Commentary.

[261] *AL.*, Vol. II, p. 223. Commentary.

[262] *AL.*,Vol. II, p. 355. Commentary. According to a footnote 'Cin' is explained in Cormac's Glossary to mean five sheets of parchment.

[263] *AL.*, Vol. II, p. 381. Commentary.

[264] For some examples see *A.L.* Vol. II, pp. 397, 399, 405.

[265] Ní Dhonnchadha, 'An Address to a Student of Law', p. 169.

[266] *Ibid.*

in a very different environment. What is significant is the choice to use tradition or old texts which are labelled traditional.

Biblical writers and exegetes made a similar use of the past in the formative stages of what has come to be known as the Bible. After a period of collecting a growing number of 'sacred' texts there was a perceived necessity to interpret them. This was not only to make the language understandable and the texts consistent and 'perfect', but to give them a bearing on the present.[267] Kugel says of the constant use of the past in the books of the Bible:

> ...the past was everywhere. It was what explained the present, and was the standard by which the present was to be judged and upon which future hopes were to be based; and it was legitimacy.[268]

The archeological evidence from the Persian period presents a striking parallel with Ireland where a deliberate decision to revive the 'past' appears to have been made. Seals found from the early part of the period (before the mid-fifth century) are the same as those found throughout the Persian empire. From the mid-fifth century to the conquest of the area by Alexander over a century later there occurs a change in the material finds. Coins, seals and impressions are found inscribed with the name 'Yehud' in Aramaic script and in old Hebrew script. Moves to reintroduce the system of weights used before the Babylonian conquest seem also to have been made. While Kugel says the connection these have with the political reality of the time cannot yet be determined, it seems there was a growing focus on the glories of past days.

> ...[T]hese findings from the material culture of Persian Judea only support the impression provided by biblical texts that the great days of the preexilic monarchy continued to serve as a model for national revival and as the focus of hopes for the future.[269]

He makes the following pivotal connection:

> The significance of this interest in the past for the course of biblical interpretation should be clear. For where was the past to be found?...*The past was in texts*, and if the past was that to which the exiles were returning, then those texts had to be studied in their tiniest details. More than this, the

---

[267] James L. Kugel, 'Early Interpretation: The Common Background of Late Forms of Biblical Exegesis', in Kugel and Greer, *Early Biblical Interpretation*, The Westminster Press, Philadelphia, 1986 p. 51.

[268] *Ibid.*, p. 36.

[269] *Ibid*, p. 37.

texts had to be...interpreted. That is, the past was not approached in the spirit of antiquarianism but for what message it might yield, and this is necessarily predicated on an interpretative stance, indeed a willingness to deviate from the texts' plain sense. The words of prophets were to be "translated" into present day significance, referred to (and sometimes distorted) in order to support to a particular view of the present, or a program for the future.[270]

This was all based, he says, on a 'belief that sacred texts have a bearing on the present.'[271]

The similarity of this Biblical example with the situation in Ireland from the fourteenth century onward is clear. The seemingly deliberate decision to continue the production of manuscripts in twelfth-century style, and based on twelfth-century and older material, at the time of a revival of Irish political fortunes, gives some indication that this revival was focussed on the greatness of the past. And like the Biblical exiles, for the Irish, the past was to be found in texts. Extensive interpretative activity was carried out on the Irish law texts as we have seen. The methods of gloss and commentary used were ones that allowed for shaping of the present and the future under the guise of adherence to the past. And this past provided legitimacy.

The question as to who has the right to interpret is also important. It is significant that the interpretation of the past is through *written* legal texts. For the process of writing is fundamentally about power relationships. Goodrich points out that it is a historically constant feature of writing that it is linked with the ruling classes. He says:

The point to be made is that written law is an early and exemplary form of writing and it should not come as a surprise if legal writings, codes and codifications, share many of the features of the early bonding of writing, power and knowledge.[272]

The power of writing is even greater in a society such as Ireland with a largely oral culture.

Writing in such cultures was always the monopoly of a restricted élite class and the reduction of oral to written law served to maintain the power and

---

[270] *Ibid.*, pp. 37-38.

[271] *Ibid.*, p. 38.

[272] Goodrich, *Reading the Law*, p. 23.

status of the literate classes within cultures where literacy was not widespread.[273]

Literacy was restricted to the élite. The power of writing lay also in the mechanics of manuscript production. The manuscripts only came to be produced, and the old texts interpreted, because of particular social and political relationships. Thus the links between interpretation, the interpreter, the social and political context are crucial to an understanding of the manuscripts. These necessarily require an explanation of the further link of power and legitimacy.

LAW, LEGITIMACY AND THE POLITICAL ÉLITE

The Irish legal families were closely connected with the newly emergent ruling families. In recognising this I believe that we should see the law manuscripts and their concentration on the past in the context of their role in legitimising these ruling families and the view of Irish society and Irish history that they were keen to promote. Donnchadh O'Corráin has already demonstrated such a function in the role of the learned classes, especially the lawyers, during the pre-Norman moves towards national unity as more power became concentrated in the hands of fewer families. As he describes, the role of the learned classes in this period was to legitimate the claims of these increasingly powerful families.[274] He suggests historians have made methodological errors in their approach specifically to Irish society and law in immediate pre-Norman Ireland. And these errors, I believe, extend into the analysis of the later period. On the general level he posits:

...historians have been deceived by the apparently static picture of Irish society presented them in the sources and, as a result, they have been insensitive to those shifts of emphasis and nuances of expression which indicate change in institutions and political and social innovations in society as a whole.[275]

He asserts that this is especially the case in Ireland:

...where the bulk of the early historical sources are literary and highly conventionalised products of specialist learned classes, retainers of the

---

[273] *Ibid.*, p. 27.
[274] O'Corráin, 'Nationality and Kingship', p. 12.
[275] *Ibid.*, p. 12.

contemporary holders of power, who were at pains to legitimise all change by giving it the sanction of immemorial custom and who ruthlessly reshaped the past to justify the present.[276]

The learned classes actively propagated the fiction of continuity and unchanged tradition.

Kim McCone says that there are many examples in medieval Irish literature that show 'the importance attached to the past as a sanction for present realities and aspirations.'[277] McCone argues that much of early Irish law is consistent with, and often drawn from, Christianity. However in the story of Patrick it is said that the laws of the Irish were already in place before the coming of Christianity: they needed only to be polished and brought in to line with Christianity by Patrick.[278] McCone argues that

> ...this construct made it possible to develop a 'native' historical typology in which Christianity represented the natural or logical fulfilment of pre-existing trends and traits in Irish history and society rather than a rude intrusion from outside. The potentially uncomfortable break between the pre-Christian past and the Christian present could thus be minimised and the integration of both phases into an essentially unitary mytho-historical model facilitated....Indeed, a combination of mythical interest in the remote past with the needs of historical typology presumably accounts for the well known early Irish juristic practice of seeking and often enough, no doubt, inventing legal precedents in the actions of important figures from their pre-Patrician 'Old Testament'.[279]

And so once again we see the practice of achieving change under the guise of the authority of the past. McCone further argues that this was very convenient for clerics who, by saying that a particular rule derived from the *senchas* in the time before Patrick, could give the prestige of the ancients to innovations they had made.[280] This he argues was generally promoted through most medieval Irish texts. McCone claims that they all:

> ...seem to be explicitly or implicitly anchored in an ideological and historical continuum stretching back from the present, via the various invasions and migrations supposed to have affected Ireland and her rulers' ancestors, to the flood and thence to the creation of the world. This scheme daringly represented Patrick's fifth-century mission to Ireland as a small

---

[276] *Ibid.*, p. 13.

[277] Mc Cone, *Pagan Past and Christian Present*, p. 105.

[278] *Ibid.*, p. 105.

[279] *Ibid.*, p. 106.

[280] *Ibid.*, p. 106.

scale re-enactment of Christ's appearance in the world to bring the Old Testament law and prophets, including history, to fulfilment in the New. Historical typology could then accommodate the pagan past to the Christian present by viewing it as an Irish 'Old Testament' perfected rather than abrogated by the national apostle's Christian dispensation. In this way all Irish legal, genealogical and mytho-historical *senchus*, whether set in the pre- or post-Patrician era, could embody a broadly identical set of contemporary values and customs represented as essentially immutable but in fact adjusted and readjusted to the Church's ongoing interaction with current social and political realities.[281]

The past had a great attraction for the Irish learned and ruling classes. Robin Chapman Stacey[282] argues that, for Irish and Welsh scholars for our period of discussion, the lawbooks were regarded as historical texts to be manipulated and preserved, to create a picture of the past which they, themselves, could understand. Nicholls makes similar observations. He says we must be careful not to allow the widely accepted view of a static late medieval Irish society to allow us to believe in a continuous Irish tradition stretching from this late medieval period back to the 'classical' past. This view, asserts Nicholls, was the work of the learned classes attempting consciously to create a justification for the newly emerged Irish lords; the learned classes worked 'with an eye to the present, of what they imagined the past to have been.'[283] Not only had there been a break in tradition, but many of the newly emergent lordships had no pre-invasion antecedents – in some cases links were being created with the past where none existed.[284]

A sense of continuity with the legal past was also promoted in the legislative activity of the Irish lords. Katharine Simms is of the opinion that there is little contemporary evidence for much legislative involvement of later medieval rulers, although there is some evidence of infrequent legislation by rulers. Simms provides several examples. In the fourteenth-century tract, *The Miracles of Senán*, we are told that:

> ...An ordinance and law was set up...that
> if any man should slay another in the land,
> and the full eric was not got from him,
> that it should be exacted from his family,

---

[281] *Ibid.*, p. 256.

[282] Stacey, *Lawbooks and Legal Enforcement in Medieval Ireland and Wales*, p. 19.

[283] Nicholls, 'Anglo-French Ireland and After', p. 392.

[284] *Ibid.*, p. 393.

and if it were not obtained from them,
it was to be exacted from his *tuath*....[285]

Clearer information is to be found on legislative activity of a later ruler of East Bréifne, Eoghan O Raighilligh who died in 1449:

> It is this Eoghan who, with lay and ecclesiastic consent composed the statutes by which the men of Bréifne abide.[286]

Despite these examples, Simms believes the reason for the paucity of legislation was the adherence to the fiction that the corpus of Irish law was unchanging. Any new ordinances that were issued were said merely to be explaining or defining the law as it already existed.[287] Thus the legal fictions promoted by the Irish jurists were a source of authority and legitimacy for the ordinances of rulers as well as for the 'law' applied by the jurists.

Nerys Patterson links manuscript production and major political change in her analysis of three sixteenth-century manuscripts containing the psuedo-historical prologue to the *Senchas Már*.[288] She considers the manuscripts in the political context in which they were produced, linking them to specific areas and dates and particular families and their legal interests. The scribal work, mainly of the O'Doran family, occurs at a period of rapid political change – defeat of Gaelic resistance and the Anglicization of government – in the areas where the O'Dorans functioned. One of the associated changes in Irish practice was abandonment of the system of paying fines for homicide and the adoption of capital punishment for this and lesser crimes. Patterson concludes:

> That they circulated, and possibly revived, the old traditions of PHP [which supported capital punishment] as a defense of this change in Irish custom – and simultaneously as a defence of Irish law against English criticism – seems much more probable than that they continued to copy old legal texts

---

[285] Simms, *From Kings to Warlords*, p. 76.

[286] *Ibid.*, p.76. Simms says the use of the English word 'statutes' (na statuide) suggests a conscious imitation of English parliamentary legislation.

[287] *Ibid.*, p. 77.

[288] Nerys Patterson, 'Gaelic law and the Tudor conquest of Ireland: the social background of the sixteenth century recensions of the psuedo-historical Prologue to the *Senchas Már*', *Irish Historical Studies*, Vol. XXVII No. 107 (May 1991), pp. 193-215.

for their antiquarian value (as has been alleged) in the midst of the disintegration of their society and their profession.[289]

USES OF THE PAST: AN ANTHROPOLOGICAL PERSPECTIVE

Eugenia Shanklin, an American anthropologist studying 'tradition' in twentieth-century Donegal, identifies four major uses of tradition: as a sanction for innovation or new customs; as a storage device for preserving important components of the behavioural or ecological system; as a way of identifying people who share a common heritage and so providing a source of ethnic identity and as a way of comparing the 'glorious past' with the realities of the present.[290] These four features are apparent to a lesser or greater degree in each of the ways the lawyers and their law manuscripts use the past for the present.

The most basic way in which the jurists use the past is by basing gloss and commentary on ancient authoritative texts. The old text would be manipulated through use of analogy to bring new laws, which had arisen in a changed social and cultural context, into accordance with the old law. Binchy gives an example of this process in his edition of *Coibnes Uisci Thairidne*.[291] Binchy states that he included both the gloss and commentary because they provide evidence of legal change 'either by their obvious unfamiliarity with the institutions described or by their efforts to fit the rules of their own day into the obsolete framework of the earlier period'.[292] Similar efforts were made, claims Binchy, at an earlier stage in production of the text itself.

> [The rules of rotation] were first worked out independently in the schools to meet a situation (which doubtless arose often in practice) where a group of neighbours between the 'source' and the 'pond' (inclusive) collaborated in erecting a mill and providing it with water. The comparison with the kin-groups can only represent an afterthought, an attempt by some jurist, perhaps the compiler of CU himself, to find a traditional basis for a relatively new arrangement.[293]

---

[289] *Ibid.*, p. 215.

[290] Eugenia Shanklin, *Donegal's Changing Traditions: An Ethnographic Study*, Gordon and Breach Science Publishers, New York, 1985 p. 17.

[291] Binchy, 'Irish Law Tracts Re-edited: I. Coibnes Uisci Thairidne', p. 68.

[292] *Ibid.*, p. 53.

[293] *Ibid.*, p. 68. Although Rolf Baumgarten argues that the kinship metaphors 'are critically applied, and they are as good and as relevant as metaphors and analogues

This search for a traditional basis, the framing of new laws in the framework of old ones, is particularly significant. It is interesting that the ancient laws of Israel, which are cited in the Hebrew Bible, had such an independent existence and recognised authority that when later writers wished to promulgate new laws, rather than starting anew, they would recombine and reuse old laws even if this was impractical and awkward.[294] That is, greater authority would accrue to these laws through their link with antiquity. Arguably the continued use of the past through the adherence to ancient laws was for the Irish jurists a similar search for legitimacy and authority.

Through the links between the Irish revival and Irish manuscript production, we may also see a wish to preserve those elements of Irish culture which were distinctive. Whether or not these distinctive elements were preserved in 'the way they had always existed' is not relevant; it is enough simply that this claim was made and that it was thought important to make it.

Providing a common ethnic identity when that very identity is called into question by the presence of people of a very different background, must also have been an important reason for the use of the past by the Irish. Establishing a commonality of interests would be important within a group seeking to resist another and particularly important, as I have been arguing, when it is trying to re-establish itself. This re-establishment involved much innovation in a very changed political, social and cultural context, and so it would have been of crucial importance to the interests of the ruling and learned classes that they appear as part of a continuous and great tradition. A similar phenomenon was perhaps at work in the revival of study of the codification of Justinian in late medieval Europe. The *Corpus Iuris* was extensively glossed

> ...to make the Roman law available for legal practice, as though the codification of Justinian had never ceased to be in force.[295]

According to Koschaker

> This idea was not only deeply rooted in Italian consciousness but was vigorously promoted by the German emperors who would naturally benefit

---

generally are in early Irish legal texts'. Rolf Baumgarten, 'The Kindred Metaphors in "Bechbretha" and "Coibnes Uisci Thairidne" ', p. 325.

[294] Kugel, 'Early Interpretation', p. 17.

[295] Franklin, *Jean Bodin*, p. 8.

from a sense of continuity with Rome. Barbarossa, on one occasion, even spoke of "my predecessors Constantine, Valentinian, Justinian".[296]

Finally, by comparing the 'glorious past' with the present, the ideal to which Irish society should be aspiring to is thrown into sharp relief. This has some similarities with Biblical activity in Hellenic and post-Hellenic times. In Hellenic and post-Hellenic times there was much activity directed toward 'Biblicising' the present. Words of the present or near future were put into the mouths of a figure from the Biblical past, stories of the present were told in an archaic Hebrew style and using purposely archaic or awkward language. Kugel sees this as symptomatic of an 'uneasiness at the gap between the Biblical ideal and the political reality.'[297]

> ...contact with Hellenism had proven decisive in both its positive and negative aspects. It provided a wealth of new ideas and techniques that helped to shape Jewish attitudes to their own ancient writings and influenced, as well, the interpretation of those writings. At the same time, resistance to Hellenization focussed the gaze of some Jews squarely on the past and on the ways of their fathers, and this provided the impetus for ever greater interest in the ancient texts and their significance.[298]

A similar phenomenon was probably at work in Ireland. The coming of the Anglo-Normans and their very obvious and threatening presence must have brought the Irish ruling and learned classes into direct contemplation of their past. A focus on the past, of the great society they were seeking to preserve or indeed to revive is to be expected. The comment on the practice of Irish law by Sir Thomas Cusack to the Privy Council in 1541, although undoubtedly imbued with Tudor bias, seems quite to the point. He says:

> ...and the inferior persons could have no right against the lord of the country, for the judge would give no judgment against the Lord, but by his own assent, and by such means kept the poor people in bondage and poverty, so that they knew no law, but the same, which caused them so long to stray from the kings majesty, for lack of knowledge of a law.[299]

---

[296] Quoted in *Ibid.*, p. 8, n.5.

[297] Kugel, Early Interpretation', pp. 47-48.

[298] *Ibid.*, p. 50.

[299] 'Sir Thomas Cusack to the Privy Council in England 1541' in Constantia Maxwell, *Irish History from Contemporary Sources, 1509-1610*, George Allen and Unwin Ltd., London, 1923 p. 114.

CONCLUSION

The past was obviously of great importance to the Irish and this, I have argued, was directed toward the present and the future. The Irish law texts as 'recordings' of the past were of intrinsic importance to those who continued to produce them and those who were patrons to this production.

I would argue this on the basis that a central anxiety of this period (explicit or implicit), may be seen as the establishment of authority. That is, legitimising the power of the re-emergent élite. The strategies and politics of this élite had changed so that a king's or a leader's power was largely dependent on military might, increasingly supplied by mercenary forces. The significance of the interrelationship of major legal families with politically (and consequently militarily) powerful families is that the jurists had an important role in transforming the power of their patrons into a more far reaching and acceptable authority. As in the pre-Norman days they were acting as the political theorists of the kings, constructing a legitimacy whereby the power of the political élite was unquestionably part of the natural state of things. And on a more self-interested level, much of their activity may be seen as a bid to secure a position for themselves as the uncontested purveyors of an expanded and reconstructed legal system. With reference to the sense of continuity with the great past and the legitimacy that this provides, one may only suppose the production of law manuscripts based on ancient canonical texts to have been of importance in a period of revival and then cultural and political survival.

VI. CONCLUSION

The copying, compiling and composing activity of the law manuscripts was a use of the past. Yet it was not the use of the past for the past's sake and hence the antiquarianism claimed by the received view; it was a use of the past for the purposes of the present and future. The Irish jurists argued strongly for the immutability and unchanging quality of their texts, and the law as revealed in these texts. However, inevitable social and cultural changes had overtaken the texts, and the old law existed in a changed context. The work of the jurists allowed the old law, representing the past, to continue to exist in the present.

The later jurists adopted a strict exegetical technique which I have already compared with that used for interpretation of the Bible and late medieval Canon and Roman law. The idea at the basis of this technique is very similar to the idea of interpretation in a formalist legal analysis. That is, it implies or assumes that there is an original, immutable meaning in the text, a meaning which this interpretative activity can recover. By insisting on this immutability of meaning, the technique implies that interpretative activity does no more than 'find' a legal meaning which already exists. The illusion in created that this process, and the application of this meaning to a legal problem, is thereby mechanical. The law is thus seen by the society in which it operates as authoritative, separate and neutral.

On a practical level, the continued adherence to the old texts while keeping them relevant in a changed society required a legal profession trained in the legal techniques necessary for manipulating the facade of unchangingness. The ability of the legal system to change through interpretation relies on the system maintaining a supply of lawyers trained to interpret. The aim of legal education is to produce interpreters committed to the formalist view of interpretation. It must inculcate this view of law into the potential lawyer, to introduce them to a language and methodology which stress that legal meaning is self-contained and that interpretation is potentially objective. In this way their activity may change the law, yet maintain its (and consequently their) authority. For the formalist approach to legal interpretation allows old texts to remain meaningful and, crucially, authoritative in the present.

The legitimacy of the legal profession, and that of the ruling classes whose interests the profession served and shared, relied also on a strong connection with the authority of the past. The claim to authority came through the use of the past. In a sense the Irish jurists, like the Irish learned classes generally, had a fixation with the past. Yet rather than being deceived into thinking theirs was a static society or, knowing that it was not, condemning them for not openly adjusting, we are challenged to inquire as to how the jurists were using the past. This use of the past, as I have argued, was very much centred in the present. The jurists were arguably legitimising the political élite: making acceptable, even 'natural', power based on military might.

These conclusions can only be tentative, however, and furthermore would require much greater attention to the sources – particularly their methods and their historical and political contexts – than can be paid here. The dating of the later medieval material, as far as this is possible, would obviously be invaluable. Nevertheless, I believe that if we change the perspective from which we regard the texts, and alter our expectations and readings of their political content and information, they may provide us with more knowledge of the later medieval period than has been thought hitherto. That is, I believe that scholarship for this period would more usefully be directed towards questioning not what these manuscripts can transparently tell us about law in late medieval Ireland, but rather what the role of these manuscripts was in this society. If we can begin from the reasonable but lamentably discounted assumption that the manuscripts had an important role, centred in the present, we may come to a better understanding of them, and the profession and the society which produced them. I believe that when these Irish law manuscripts are seen in the context of the politics and society of their time, then they assume great interest and significance independently of the information they contain about early Irish law.

For the fact that the law texts are seen primarily as a source for law and society in early medieval Ireland is problematic. The evidence for the earlier period only survives in later, highly interpreted and reconstructed manuscripts. If, as I have argued, the interpretative activity of the later jurists was directed towards the present, then what we know of the earlier period must in some way be affected by this realisation. Of course, the argument that the scribal activity of the later jurists was merely antiquarian avoids, and even ignores this probability. For if the manuscripts were not being used for any practical purposes, and were in effect an activity completely separated from everyday affairs, the likelihood of the jurists taking a particularly active part in the reconstruction of meaning recedes (as distinct from changes wrought through their 'mistakes' and 'incomprehension'). If, however, one does not accept that the later jurists were merely antiquarian in their scribal activity but, as I have argued, were engaged in an activity very much centred in the present, then this later period of Irish law and Irish law transmission, assumes a position of importance, not merely for its own time, but also for the earlier period. What I have argued for leads to a re-politicising of the late medieval law manuscripts. It argues that the presumed 'stasis' of the texts must be seen in terms of the changes occurring in Irish society, and the sites for law manuscript production in the late medieval period. This argument requires that the links between this production and the patronage of powerful local rulers be investigated and that inquiry be made into the effect of this patronage on the manuscript.

In using modern interpretative and legal theory, the scribal activity of the later jurists cannot be seen as entirely removed from its society, as an untainted fascination with the past. Indeed, what this theory does is challenge the very notion of antiquarianism. For history seems to teach that there can never be an apolitical use of the past. Any use of the past, any textual activity, is highly political and culturally motivated and the law manuscripts are no exception. They are, however, fascinating for the objectivity and neutrality they so strongly promote. Seeking an understanding of the politics of this textual production, and their proposed stasis against such a vigorously changing background may, I believe, allow us to perceive the work of the late medieval Irish jurists, not as antiquarianism, but as a highly politically charged activity. If we fail to understand this, the rhetoric of the jurists has been all too effective in persuading not only the late medieval but also their twentieth-century readers, and at least some of their political aims continue to be served: attention is directed away from their activity and toward the 'authoritative' canonical texts. Modern textual and legal theory, however, asks us to fix our gaze squarely on the late medieval jurists and examine them and their 'secondary' activity: to examine, not what they claim to have been doing, but what we might 'interpret' them as having done.

Bibliography

Abbott, T.K. and Gwynn, E.J., *Catalogue of Manuscripts*, Library of Trinity College, Dublin, Dublin, 1921.

Baker, J.H., 'The Inns of Court and Legal Doctrine', in Charles Edwards, T.M., Owen, Morfydd E. and Walters, D.B. (eds.), *Lawyers and Laymen*, University of Wales Press, Cardiff, 1986.

Bakhtin, M.M., *The Dialogic Imagination*, (Edited by Michael Holquist, translated by Caryl and Michael Holquist) University of Texas Press, Austin, 1981.

Baumgarten, Rolf, 'The Kindred Metaphors in Bechbretha and Coibnes Uisci Thairidne', *Peritia* 4 (1985) 307–27.

Binchy, D.A., 'Ancient Irish Law', *Irish Jurist*, 1 (1966) 84–92.

Binchy, D.A., 'Irish History and Irish Law: II', *Studia Hibernica*, 16 (1976) 7–45.

Binchy, D.A., 'Irish Law Tracts Re-edited: I. Coibnes Uisci Thairidne', *Eriu*, XVII (1955) 52–85.

Binchy, D.A., 'Lawyers and Chroniclers', in Brian O'Cuív (ed.), *Seven Centuries of Irish Learning*, Radio Eireann Thomas Davis Lectures, The Stationery Office, 1961.

Binchy, D.A., 'Bretha Nemed', *Eriu*, XVII (1955) 4–6.

Binchy, D.A., *Corpus Iuris Hibernici* (Vols. 1–6), Institúid Ard-Léinn Bhaile Atha Cliath, Baile Atha Cliath, 1978.

Blake, Martin J., 'Two Irish Brehon scripts: with notes on the Mac Egan family', *Journal of the Galway Archeological and Historical Society*, 6 (1909) 1–8.

Breatnach, Liam, 'Lawyers in early Ireland', in Hogan, Daire and Osborough, W.N. (eds.), *Brehons, Serjeants and Attorneys: Studies in the History of the Irish Legal Profession*, Irish Academic Press, 1990.

[Breatnach, Liam, *A Companion to the Corpus Iuris Hibernici*, Dublin Institute for Advanced Studies, Dublin, 2005.]

Burke, John, *Osborn's Concise Law Dictionary*, 6th Ed., Sweet and Maxwell, London, 1976.

Campbell, Marion, 'Unending desire: Sidney's reinvention of petrarchan form in Astrophil and Stella', *Sir Philip Sidney and the Interpretation of Renaissance Culture: the Poet in his time and ours*, Waller and Moore (eds.), Croom Helm, London, 1984.

Cosgrove, Art, *Late Medieval Ireland, 1370–1541*, Helicon Ltd, Dublin, 1981.

Costello, Thomas B., 'The Ancient Law School of Park, Co. Galway', *Journal of the Galway Archeological and Historical Society*, 19 (1940) 89–100.

Curtis, E. and Mc Dowell, R.B., *Irish Historical Documents, 1172–1922*, Methuen and Co. Ltd., London, 1943.

Curtis, E., *A History of Medieval Ireland from 1086–1513*, (2nd Ed.), Methuen, London, 1938.

Davies, R.R., 'The Administration of Law in Medieval Wales: The Role of the Ynad Cwmwd (Judex Patrie)', in Charles Edwards, T.M., Owen, Morfydd E. and Walters, D.B. (eds.), *Lawyers and Laymen*, University of Wales Press, Cardiff, 1986.

Dillon, Myles, 'Literary Activity in the pre-Norman Period', in O'Cuiv, *Seven Centuries of Irish Learning, 1000–1700*, Published for Radio Eireann by the Stationery Office, 1961.

Dumville, David, 'Language, Literature and Law in Medieval Ireland: Some Questions of Transmission', *Cambridge Medieval Celtic Studies*, 9 (Summer 1985) 91–98.

Frame, Robin, *English Lordship in Ireland 1318–1361*, Clarendon Press, Oxford, 1982.

Franklin, Julian H., *Jean Bodin and the Sixteenth Century Revolution in the Methodology of Law and History*, London, 1963.

Goodrich, Peter, 'Law and Language: An Historical and Critical Introduction', *Journal of Law and Society*, Vol. 11, No. 2 (Summer 1984) 173–206.

Goodrich, Peter, *Reading the Law: A Critical Introduction to Legal Method and Techniques*, Basil Blackwell Ltd., Oxford, 1986.

Gwynn, E.J., 'An Old-Irish tract on the Priviledges and Responsibilities of Poets', *Eriu*, XIII (1942) 1–12.

Hancock, O'Mahoney, Richey, Hennessy and Atkinson (eds.), *Ancient Laws of Ireland*, vols. 1–6, Alexander Thom & Co. Ltd., Dublin, 1865–1901.

Hand, G.J., *English Law in Ireland 1290–1324*, Cambridge University Press, London, 1967.

Hayes-McCoy, G.A., 'Gaelic Society in Ireland in the late Sixteenth Century', *Historical Studies*, 4 (1963) 45–61.

Henry, Françoise and Marsh-Micheli, Geneviève, 'Manuscripts and Illuminations, 1169–1603', in Cosgrove (ed.), *A New History of Ireland II: Medieval Ireland, 1169–1534*, Clarendon Press, Oxford, 1987.

Kelleher, John V., 'Early Irish History and Pseudo-History', *Studia Hibernica*, 3 (1963) 113–127.

Kelly, Fergus, *A Guide to Early Irish Law*, Dublin Institute for Advanced Studies, Dublin, 1988.

Kugel, James L., 'Early Interpretation: The Common Background of Late Forms of Biblical Exegesis', in Kugel and Greer, *Early Biblical Interpretation*, The Westminster Press, Philadelphia, 1986.

Mac Neill, Eoin, 'Prolegomena to a study of the Ancient Laws of Ireland' ed. with Introduction and Footnotes by D.A. Binchy, *The Irish Jurist*, 2 (1967) 106–115.

Mac Niocaill, Gearóid, 'Aspects of Irish Law in the Late Thirteenth Century', *Historical Studies*, X (1976) 25–42.

Mac Niocaill, Gearóid, 'Jetsam, Treasure Trove and the Lord's Share in Medieval Ireland', *The Irish Jurist*, 6 (1971) 103–110.

Mac Niocaill, Gearóid, 'Notes on Litigation in Late Irish Law', *The Irish Jurist*, 2 (1967) 299–307.

Mac Niocaill, Gearóid, 'The contact of Irish and common law', *N.I. Legal Quart.*, XXIII (1972) 16–23.

Mac Niocaill, Gearóid, 'The interaction of laws', in James Lydon (ed.), *The English in Medieval Ireland*, Royal Irish Academy, 1984.

Macnamara, George U., 'The O'Davorens of Cahermachnaughten, Burren, Co. Clare', *North Munster Archeological Society Journal*, 2 (1912–1913), 63–93, 149–64, 194–201.

Maine, Sir Henry Sumner, *Ancient Law: Its connection with the early history of society and its relation to modern ideas*, Oxford University Press, London, 1861 (1954 reprint).

Mazzeo, Joseph, *Varieties of Interpretation*, University of Notre Dame Press, Notre Dame, 1978.

McCone, Kim, *Pagan Past and Christian Present in Early Irish Literature*, An Sagart, 1990 (1991 reprint).

Miller, L. and Power, E., *Holinsheds Irish Chronicle 1577*, Dublin, 1979.

Ní Dhonnchadha, Máirín, 'An Address to a Student of Law', in O Corráin, Breatnach and McCone (eds.), *Sages, Saints and Storytellers: Celtic Studies in Honour of Professor James Carney*, An Sagart, Maynooth, 1989.

Nicholls, K.W., 'Anglo-French Ireland and After', *Peritia*, 1 (1982) 370–403.

Nicholls, Kenneth, *Gaelic and Gaelicised Ireland in the Middle Ages*, Gill and Macmillan, Dublin, 1972.

O'Corráin, D., Breatnach, L. and Breen, A., 'The Laws of the Irish', *Peritia*, 3 (1984) 382–438.

O'Corráin, Donnchadh, 'Nationality and Kingship in Pre-Norman Ireland', in *Nationality and the Pursuit of National Independence*, Apple Tree Press, Belfast, 1978.

O'Donovan, John (ed. & trans.), *Annals of the Kingdom of Ireland by the Four Masters*, Hodges, Smith, & Co., Dublin, 1854. (A.M.S. Press, Inc. N.Y. 1966).

O'Grady, Standish Hayes, *Catalogue of Irish Manuscripts in the British Museum*, Vol. 1, London, 1926.

O'Neill, Timothy, *The Irish Hand*, The Dolmen Press, Dublin, 1984.

O'Sullivan, Anne and O'Sullivan, William, 'Edward Lhuyd's Collection of Irish Manuscripts', *Transactions of the Honourable Society of Cymmrodorion*, 1962.

Orpen, G.H., *Ireland Under the Normans*, Clarendon Press, Oxford, 1920. (Reprinted 1968).

Patterson, Nerys, 'Brehon Law in Late Medieval Ireland: "Antiquarian and Obsolete" or "Traditional and Functional"?', *Cambridge Medieval Celtic Studies*, 17 (Summer 1989) 43–63.

Patterson, Nerys, 'Gaelic law and the Tudor conquest of Ireland: the social background of the sixteenth century recensions of the psuedo-historical Prologue to the Senchas Már', *Irish Historical Studies*, Vol. XXVII No. 107 (May 1991) 193-215.

Richter, Michael, *Medieval Ireland: The Enduring Tradition*, Macmillan Education, 1988.

Ryan SJ, John, 'The Historical Background' in O'Cuiv, *Seven Centuries of Irish Learning, 1000–1700*, Published for Radio Eireann by the Stationery Office, 1961.

Schauer, Frederick, 'An Essay on Constiitutional Language', in Sanford Levinson and Stephen Mailloux (eds.), *Interpreting Law and Literature: A Hermeneutic Reader*, Northwestern University Press, Evanston, IL, 1988.

Shanklin, Eugenia, *Donegal's Changing Traditions: An Ethnographic Study*, Gordon and Breach Science Publishers, New York, 1985.

Silverman, Eric Kline, 'Clifford Geertz: Towards a More "Thick" Understanding', in Tilley, Christopher (ed.), *Reading Material Culture: Structuralism, Hermeneutics and Post-Structuralism*, Basil Blackwell, Oxford, 1990.

Simms, Katharine, 'The brehons of later medieval Ireland', in Hogan, Daire and Osborough, W.N. (eds.), *Brehons, Serjeants and Attorneys: Studies in the History of the Irish Legal Profession*, Irish Academic Press, 1990.

Simms, Katharine, 'The Legal Position of Irish Women in the Later Middle Ages', *The Irish Jurist*, 10 (1975) 96–111.

Simms, Katharine, *From Kings to Warlords*, The Boydell Press, Suffolk, 1987.

Stacey, Robin Chapman, *Lawbooks and Legal Enforcement in Medieval Ireland and Wales*, Unpublished PhD dissertation, Yale University, May 1986.

Watt, J.A., 'Approaches to the History of Fourteenth Century Ireland' in Cosgrove (ed.), *A New History of Ireland II: Medieval Ireland, 1169–1534*, Clarendon Press, Oxford, 1977.

White, James Boyd, *Heracles' Bow: Essays on the Rhetoric and Poetics of the Law*, University of Wisconsin Press, Wisconsin, 1985.

White, James Boyd, *Justice as Translation: An Essay in Cultural and Legal Criticism*, University of Chicago Press, Chicago, 1990.

Index